GRAMMATICAL EVOLUTION

Evolutionary Automatic Programming in an Arbitrary Language

GENETIC PROGRAMMING SERIES

Series Editor

John Koza
Stanford University

Also in the series:

GENETIC PROGRAMMING AND DATA STRUCTURES: Genetic Programming + Data Structures = Automatic Programming! *William B. Langdon*; ISBN: 0-7923-8135-1

AUTOMATIC RE-ENGINEERING OF SOFTWARE USING GENETIC PROGRAMMING, *Conor Ryan;* ISBN: 0-7923-8653-1

DATA MINING USING GRAMMAR BASED GENETIC PROGRAMMING AND APPLICATIONS, *Man Leung Wong and Kwong Sak Leung;* ISBN: 0-7923-7746-X

The cover image was generated using Genetic Programming and interactive selection. Anargyros Sarafopoulos created the image, and the GP interactive selection software.

GRAMMATICAL EVOLUTION

Evolutionary Automatic Programming in an Arbitrary Language

by

Michael O'Neill
University of Limerick, Ireland

Conor Ryan
University of Limerick, Ireland

KLUWER ACADEMIC PUBLISHERS
Boston / Dordrecht / London

Distributors for North, Central and South America:
Kluwer Academic Publishers
101 Philip Drive; Assinippi Park
Norwell, Massachusetts 02061 USA
Telephone (781) 871-6600
Fax (781) 681-9045
E-Mail: kluwer@wkap.com

Distributors for all other countries:
Kluwer Academic Publishers Group
Post Office Box 322
3300 AH Dordrecht, THE NETHERLANDS
Telephone 31 78 6576 000
Fax 31 78 6576 254
E-Mail: services@wkap.nl

Electronic Services <http://www.wkap.nl>

Library of Congress Cataloging-in-Publication Data

Michael O'Neill, Conor Ryan
GRAMMATICAL EVOLUTION: Evolutionary Automatic Programming in an Arbitrary Language
ISBN: 1-4020-7444-1

Printed on acid-free paper. Printed in the United States of America.

Contents

Preface

Since man began to dream of machines that could automate not only the more mundane and laborious tasks of everyday life, but that could also improve some of the more agreeable aspects, he has turned to nature for inspiration. This inspiration has taken all sorts of forms, with inventors producing everything from Icarus-like, bird-inspired flying machines to robots based on some of the more mechanically useful human appendages.

Another inspiration that can be taken from nature is to employ its *tools*, rather than necessarily employing its *products*. In this way, the field of evolutionary computation has taken stock of the power of evolution, and applied it, albeit at a very coarse level, to problem solving. Genetic Programming, a powerful incarnation of evolutionary computation uses the artificial evolutionary process to automatically generate programs. The adoption of evolution to automatic generation of programs represents one of the most promising approaches to that holy grail of computer science, automatic programming, that is, a computer that can automatically generate a program from scratch given a high-level problem description.

Research in Genetic Programming has explored a number of program representations beyond the original Lisp S-expression syntax trees, and some of the more powerful of these incorporate a developmental strategy that transforms an embryonic state into a fully fledged adult program.

The form of Genetic Programming presented in this book, Grammatical Evolution, delves further into nature's processes at a molecular level, embracing the developmental approach, and drawing upon a number of principles that allow an abstract representation of a program to be evolved.

This abstraction enables firstly, a separation of the search and solution spaces that allow the EA search engine to be a plug-in component of the system, facilitating the exploitation of advances in EAs by GE. Secondly, this allows the evolution of programs in an arbitrary language with the representation of a program's syntax in the form of a grammar definition.

Thirdly, the existence of a degenerate genetic code is enabled, giving a many-to-one mapping, that allows the exploitation of neutral evolution to enhance the search efficiency of the EA. Fourthly, we can adopt the use of a wrapping operator that allows the reuse of genetic material during a genotype-phenotype mapping process.

This book is partly based on the Ph.D. thesis of Michael O'Neill, and reports a number of new directions in Grammatical Evolution research that are been conducted both within the confines of the University of Limerick's Biocomputing-Developmental Systems Centre where the book's authors reside, and also developments that are occurring through collaborations around the globe.

M. O'NEILL & C. RYAN

Foreword

This book is based on the PhD thesis of Michael O'Neill, but is written in a very accessible language intended for a wider audience. The authors succeed to elucidate aspects of Genetic Programming that have hitherto not been examined in such detail.

Genetic Programming (GP) was first applied seriously in expression trees of LISP-like program structures. I do not rule out the possibility that these first steps were due to the clean nature of LISP and its derivatives which made it possible to focus attention on the mechanical problem of getting evolution to go, instead of being forced to constantly observe the behavior of the underlying representation.

After the formalization of grammars through Chomsky, both the Linguistics and the Computer Science community have taken advantage of the new tools. Notably Computer Science was able to exploit Chomsky's formalism for the systematic generation of a multitude of computer languages that since populate our machines. Up to this day it is a key activity of Computer Scientists to invent new languages. It is thus very natural to ask whether Genetic Programming which intends to apply artificial evolution to the determination of computer behavior would not be best used in the realm of those structures and rules which make up computer programs.

Once it was shown that GP is possible in principle, a variety of representations appeared which exploited different aspects of the paradigm. Among these were grammars and linear strings of code. Both aspects are an active area of research in Evolutionary Computation. The use of grammatical structures for GP has recently gained much prominence through the work of the authors. In a variety of applications O'Neill and Ryan show convincing evidence that Grammatical Evolution, GE as it is abbreviated, is a lively branch of Genetic Programming.

In the distinctive words of the authors, with grammars "one is effectively using the weapon of the enemy against them". Complexity of behavior is approached from a perspective of building it up from simple rules, much as the complexity of meaning is built up from the use of grammars in natural language. At the heart of GE lies the fact that genes are only used to determine which rule is applied when, not what the rules are. Those are fixed beforehand as the grammar and provide the environment from which genes choose their "words".

Other important aspects of this work are development and linearity of code. By development in Grammatical Evolution, the process of constructing the phenotype is meant, a process strictly under control of the chosen (arbitrary) grammar. Linearity is an aspect of GE analogous to what is found in natural evolutionary systems. Instead of nucleotides, the linear sequence of genotypes is written in simple bit patterns which are interpreted appropriately. The process generates a number of phenomena also found in natural evolution, for instance the appearance (and productive use) of neutral code.

In my mind, we are just at the beginning of a thorough exploration of possibilities for artificial evolution through these processes. A great deal of Terra Incognita lies before us and is waiting to be explored. "Grammatical Evolution" is an important contribution to this undertaking. I am very glad that this book, written by two specialists, Michael O'Neill and Conor Ryan, has appeared.

Wolfgang Banzhaf

To John & Jane, and Gráinne
Michael

To Katy, my favourite distraction
Conor

Acknowledgments

It has been five years since the first Grammatical Evolution publication, and in that time, a large number of people have helped us out in all sorts of ways. We are very fortunate that many of these people have also become very good friends because of, and, in some cases, despite, working with us.

J.J. Collins was a co-author on the first GE paper and contributed a lot of GA code to the original system, while **Maarten Keijzer** has been involved in a number of our recent papers, was responsible for the work on Ripple Crossover and ALP, and contributed to many intense discussions, some of which were related to Evolutionary Computation. **Tony Brabazon** introduced us to the delights of Financial Prediction, and was involved in some of the papers that contributed to Chapter 8. **Miguel Nicolau** contributed to a number of different aspects of this work, and is currently developing GAUGE, as well as pretending that he can play the guitar. **Atif Azad** and **Ali Ansari** co-operated with the work on Chorus, as did **Alan Sheahan**, who also advised us on statistics in the book, as well as pretending that he can't play the guitar. **Mike Cattolico** was involved in the work on crossover, and made sure that we ate properly while in the US. **John O'Sullivan** was responsible for the work on comparing search strategies, and **Vladan Babovic** was a collaborator on both the Ripple Crossover and Logic Programming sections, while **Robin Matthews** collaborated on the Financial Prediction work.

Other people not directly involved in the work, but to whom we are thankful for their support and help include **Wolfgang Banzhaf**, **John Koza**, **Forrest H. Bennett III**, **Bill Langdon**, **Una-May O'Reilly**, **Norman Paterson**, **Tony Cahill** and **Jennifer Willies**.

We are also thankful to the continued support of the **Computer Science and Information Systems** department at the **University of Limerick**, past and present members of the **Biocomputing-Developmental Systems Centre** there and the staff at Kluwer, particularly the ever-patient **Melissa Fearon**.

We would like to thank our parents, families and friends for showing that there is life beyond GE.

Chapter 1

INTRODUCTION

This book is about Grammatical Evolution (GE), an approach to Genetic Programming that allows the generation of computer programs in an arbitrary language. GE exploits a rich modularity in its design that results in a highly flexible and easy to use system. GE owes this design and, consequently, its most powerful features to inspiration from biological systems. There are two main themes to the book; the first being the adoption of phenomena from molecular biology in *a simple and useful* manner, and the second being the use of grammars to specify legal structures in a search.

1. EVOLUTIONARY AUTOMATIC PROGRAMMING

Evolutionary Automatic Programming (EAP), the automatic generation of computer programs through evolutionary computation, has gained widespread popularity in the past ten to fifteen years. Much of this is due to the seminal work of John Koza on Genetic Programming (GP) (Koza, 1989; Koza, 1992).

Such has been the meteoric rise and enormous influence of GP, the term Genetic Programming is usually used to describe any Evolutionary Automatic Programming system, even those that diverge from the tree-based direct representation of Koza's GP. Grammatical Evolution is a form of Genetic Programming that differs from traditional GP in three fundamental ways; it employs linear genomes, it performs an ontogenetic mapping from the genotype to the phenotype (program) and it uses a grammar to dictate legal structures in the phenotypic space.

At the heart of any evolutionary automatic programming approach is the evolutionary algorithm engine that was first described by John Holland in (Holland, 1975) and inspired by the notions of survival of the fittest (Spencer, 1864) and natural selection (Darwin, 1859). A population of solutions is maintained, each individual of which is evaluated to determine its performance on the problem in question. The performance of an individual program on the problem is referred to as its fitness. Those individuals that have a superior performance on the task are assigned a better fitness value, and are most likely to survive by reproducing. It follows that these individuals are more likely to pass their genetic material to the next generation. This is based on the natural process of *natural selection*, in which those individuals best adapted to their environment, or, in terms of Evolutionary Computation, those individuals that are best adapted to the problem, survive to produce the following generation.

The inspiration provided by nature to the field of evolutionary computation does not cease at the level of the basic evolutionary process as outlined above. The research described in this book delves further into the treasures that recent advances in the field of Molecular Biology have revealed.

2. MOLECULAR BIOLOGY

Molecular Biology, a relatively young scientific field, has yielded many insights into the innermost workings of the fundamental units of complex organisms, the cell. Discoveries include the structure of the hereditary material deoxyribonucleic acid (DNA), the discovery of proteins and their structural units, the elucidation of the genetic code, and the complex signaling networks that exist within and between cells. Of utmost importance is what has become known as *the central dogma of Molecular Biology*. This tenet describes the processes of transcription and translation, i.e., that DNA is transcribed to messenger ribonucleic acid (mRNA), which in turn is translated into protein. Proteins are responsible for the generation of phenotypic traits, such as eye colour, and height. In terms of Evolutionary Automatic Programming this amounts to a distinction of genotype and phenotype. The separation of search and solution spaces that is achieved with the adoption of such a genotype-phenotype mapping allows practitioners of Evolutionary Automatic Programming to embrace a number of advantages that are otherwise unavailable to approaches operating directly upon phenotypic structures. A number of these advantages are explored in the context of the Grammatical Evolution system. Of particular importance is the ability to represent the phenotypic structures in a more abstract form through the use of grammars.

3. GRAMMARS

The beauty of grammars is that they provide a single mechanism that can be used to describe all manner of complex structures. Grammars can describe languages, graphs, neural networks, mathematical expressions, the manner in which molecules arrange themselves in compounds, etc. One advantage of using grammars as part of an evolutionary computation tool is that one is effectively using the weapon of the enemy against them. That is, instead of evolving a structure directly, which can attract problems such as invalid crossovers and infeasible individuals, the search is instead performed on the derivation sequence required to produce the desired structure. The more one knows about a particular problem, the more one can enrich the grammar with all manner of insider information about the problem. Importantly, the grammar simply states what *can* be done, while the search dictates what *should* be done.

A grammar is set of rules that govern how a complex structure is built up from small building blocks. When deriving a legal structure (or "sentence") for a particular grammar, one follows a *derivation* sequence , which is a sequence of choices made using the rules of the grammar. Changing the rules can change the sentences produced by the grammar. These changes can range from the minute, where only the most subtle of variation results, to the more severe, where one can bias the sentences to a particular form, to the downright dramatic, where the sentences produced bear little or no resemblance to the original products.

It is this plasticity that makes grammars so attractive as part of an Evolutionary Computation tool. Not only are they convenient methods of describing legal solutions, they can also be tuned during the course of a run in response to the system output. Furthermore, such is the flexibility of grammars, that employing a completely different grammar can make a system appear to work very differently, yet the fundamentals remain the same. This means that a tool that uses a grammatical component can be applied to an enormous set of problems, simply by changing the grammar to the appropriate type.

Grammatical Evolution evolves simple linear genomes, which are used to dictate choices in the derivation sequence. This gives a complete separation of search and solution space, where the genetic operators are applied to the binary string, after which it is mapped onto a legal phenotype. As in nature, there are no genetic operations applied to the phenotype, which means that it can be as complex as necessary, and problems such as over- and under-specification, and infeasible crossovers simply do not occur.

4. OUTLINE

Chapter 2 contains a survey of the field of Evolutionary Automatic Programming, thus putting GE into an historical context. Over the course of this chapter it will become apparent how the field has itself evolved.

Many of the more successful evolutionary algorithms are characterised by the manner in which they model phenomena from nature. Chapter 3 gives a brief overview of some of the fundamentals of Molecular Biology, and reflects on the benefits Evolutionary Automatic Programming systems could derive from this field. For example, by adopting a genotype-phenotype distinction it is possible to separate the search and solution spaces, and to preserve genetic diversity within the evolving populations, thus acting as a preventative measure against premature convergence on local optima.

A thorough description of the Grammatical Evolution system is given in chapter 4. We show how Grammatical Evolution takes note of the findings in chapters 2 and 3 and builds upon these to develop a system that is capable of generating programs in an arbitrary language.

In chapter 5, Grammatical Evolution is applied to a number of benchmark problems, and its success compared to Genetic Programming. The problems investigated are a symbolic regression problem, a symbolic integration problem, the Santa Fe trail, and the evolution of Caching Algorithms.

The next two chapters, 6 and 7, contain an in depth analysis of some of the features of Grammatical Evolution in which particular attention is focused upon the degenerate genetic code, the wrapping operator and the crossover genetic search operator. It is shown that these features play an important role in GE's success.

Chapter 8 presents some extensions and example applications of Grammatical Evolution. We then conclude with an overview, conclusions, and outline possible directions for future research.

Chapter 2

SURVEY OF EVOLUTIONARY AUTOMATIC PROGRAMMING

1. INTRODUCTION

Before conducting a survey of Evolutionary Automatic Programming, it is worth considering what we mean by the term Automatic Programming. Since the inception of a programmable computing device, researchers have sought to achieve Automatic Programming. The meaning of this term, however, has changed over time, as expectations are relative to the current technologies available (Rich and Waters, 1988).

In the early days of computing Automatic Programming referred to assemblers, that is, programs that would automatically generate the corresponding machine code from a program written in assembly language. At this time, an assembler relieved a huge burden for a programmer, automating the task of physically writing the binary codes that made up a machine code program. As time progressed, compilers for second generation programming languages such as Fortran were considered Automatic Programming. Following along the lines of the development of more sophisticated compilers came the third and fourth generation programming languages, and in the 1990's much work has been done on the automatic parallelisation of code, see for example (Foster, 1991; Lovely, 1992; Blume and Eigenmann, 1992; Ryan, 1999).

Today, Automatic Programming is in the realm of Intelligent Systems, and is perhaps best described by Arthur Samuel (Samuel, 1959) when he said

> "Tell the computer what to do, not how to do it."

In other words, we wish to be able to automatically generate a program from scratch given a high-level problem description. For this definition of Automatic Programming we must adopt the technologies of machine learning in order to achieve this goal. To date, the most successful approaches in this direction are

Genetic Programming, an Evolutionary Automatic Programming approach, and Inductive Logic Programming.

Inductive Logic Programming (ILP)(Muggleton, 1992) is an approach that combines logic programming and machine learning and typically adopts the Prolog language. The ILP approach has produced systems like FOIL (First Order Inductive Logic) (Quinlan, 1990), a natural extension of ID3, that induces decision trees.

More recently there has been work to combine the best of these two approaches, that is from ILP taking the notion of a logic program and from Evolutionary Automatic Programming the ability to evolve programs to produce a system that can evolve logic programs (Wong and Leung, 2000).

A number of attributes that an automatic programming system should possess have been identified in (Koza et al., 1999). These attributes include:

- the ability to start with a high-level problem description that results in a solution in the form of a computer program,
- the ability to automatically determine the programs size and architecture,
- the ability to automatically organise a group of instructions so that they may be re-used by a program,
- problem-independence,
- scalability to larger versions of the same problem,
- and the capability of producing results that are competitive with those produced by humans.

We will now continue by conducting a review of Evolutionary Automatic Programming as this is the area in which the work of this book lies.

2. EVOLUTIONARY AUTOMATIC PROGRAMMING

The phrase Evolutionary Automatic Programming is used to refer to those systems that adopt evolutionary computation to automatically generate computer programs, and as such includes Genetic Programming (GP) and all its variants (e.g. Binary GP, AIM GP, developmental GP). We feel that the use of the term Evolutionary Automatic Programming, instead of GP with its various interpretations, is preferable when speaking about a GP system as it is not always clear as to the differences, if any, from the traditional tree-based Koza GP approach that operates directly upon the phenotypic trees (Koza, 1992). This chapter describes the diverse array of approaches that have been adopted in this field of research and illustrate the success these techniques have enjoyed for the automatic generation of programs. We trace the evolution of this field from its humble beginnings evolving binary strings that specified a homegrown machine language, to the rich expressiveness of tree-based systems evolving Lisp S-expressions. We conclude by returning to string based systems involving evolution of C and machine code.

The field of evolutionary computation is based on the notion of biological evolution as described by Charles Darwin, that is, natural selection (Darwin, 1859) and incorporates Herbert Spencer's notion of survival of the fittest (Spencer, 1864). Given a population of individuals where each individual represents a possible solution to a particular problem (e.g. a set of parameters), each individual is evaluated to determine its performance on the problem in question. The performance of an individual program on the problem is referred to as its fitness. Those individuals that have a superior performance on the task are assigned a better fitness value, and are most likely to survive by reproducing. It follows that these individuals are more likely to pass their genetic material to the next generation. The process of selecting individuals to reproduce, or, in evolutionary computation, to solve a problem, is referred to as natural selection. The idea being that, over time, reproduction and natural selection allow the evolution of progressively more fit individuals.

An evolutionary algorithm's population must be initialised before evolution can commence; typically this is conducted in a random fashion. For example, a random number generator is often used to set each bit value of every individual in a population of a simple Genetic Algorithm. In some cases it is desirable to seed the population with previous solutions, or attempt to confer a diversity of structure upon the first generation as commonly used in Genetic Programming, where variable length tree structures are adopted.

Each cycle of an evolutionary algorithm, otherwise referred to as a generation, is typically comprised of the phases *selection*, *genetic manipulation*, *testing* and *replacement*. During selection individuals are selected to be parents based on their fitness values, that is, their performance, or lack of, at solving the target problem. Some genetic manipulation is then applied to these parents to generate children, followed by a testing phase that determines the fitness of each child solution. The replacement strategy determines how the children, parents and other members of the current population are used to create the next generation. An outline of an evolutionary algorithm can be seen below.

New generations are continuously created until the stopping criteria have been fulfilled. These are taken as being either an adequate solution has been found, or a set number of generations have elapsed.

```
Initialise Population
WHILE termination criterion not satisfied
DO
    Evaluate fitness of each individual
    Select Parents
```

```
        Apply Genetic Operators
        Create new population
    END DO
    Report best-of-run individual
```

Evolutionary computation can be thought of as being comprised of a family of algorithms loosely based on the concept of survival of the fittest. The primary members of this family are the Genetic Algorithm (GA), Evolutionary Strategies (ES), Evolutionary Programming (EP), and Genetic Programming (GP).

The boundaries of distinction between each family member are becoming increasingly blurred. Traditionally, perhaps the most distinguishing factor of each of these algorithms was the representation that was adopted. In the case of GAs, these are traditionally fixed-length binary strings, in ES real-valued vectors, in EP individuals were originally finite state machines, and in GP, Lisp S-expressions are traditionally the individuals of choice.

Current thinking suggests that, rather than concerning ourselves with distinguishing these members of the family, we should be able to combine the desirable properties from each of these approaches to suit the problem being tackled, by adopting an evolutionary algorithm (De Jong, 1999). For example, using a linear GA-like genome to evolve Lisp S-expressions.

As the main focus of this book is on Evolutionary Automatic Programming, we concentrate the following discussion on Genetic Programming and its variants. Before doing so, we will place Genetic Programming within the historical context of Evolutionary Automatic Programming.

3. ORIGIN OF THE SPECIES

The concept of evolving executable computer programs dates back to Friedberg in 1958 (Friedberg, 1958), where "random changes" (analogous to what we now call mutations) and other "routine changes"[1] were made to binary string structures. These simple machine code programs were generated to solve simple arithmetic calculations, such as the addition of two numbers. Learning was implemented by using a credit assignment approach, whereby the performance of individual instructions was monitored. As noted in this work, no account was taken of the fact that there are interdependencies between instructions.

In (Friedberg et al., 1959), two benchmark strategies for generating programs were compared for efficiency on their "learning machine" described in (Friedberg, 1958). The first strategy made small changes by modifying a couple of instructions in the machine code. The second approach involved changing all

[1] At any given time, two possible instructions are kept on record for each instruction position in the program, one of which is active. The routine or deterministic changes involve swapping the instruction that is currently active for that position to its alternative instruction.

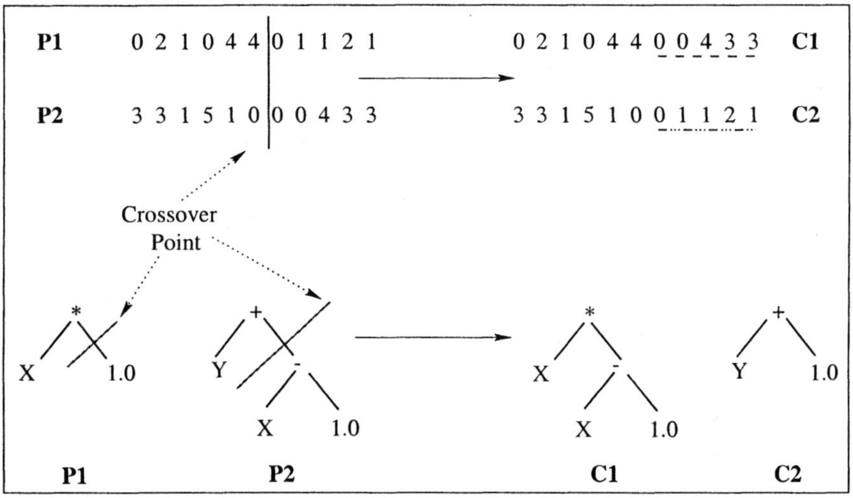

Figure 2.1. Examples of the crossover genetic operator at work. The top figure represents crossover operating on a linear string of integers, where P1 and P2 are the parents upon which a crossover point is selected. C1 and C2 are the two children produced as a result of the operator. The bottom figure represents crossover (sub-tree) as performed on tree structures.

the instructions within the code. It was found that the second, more aggressive, strategy was more efficient in terms of speed of obtaining correct programs. Results demonstrated that their original learning machine's performance was inferior to this second aggressive strategy, but on a par with the first. An attempt to improve the performance of their approach lead them to partitioning the problem into smaller sub-problems, leading to a performance that surpassed both of their benchmarks. It is worth noting that this approach adopted no notion of selection.

The next documented attempt to evolve computer programs directly was by Cramer in 1985 (Cramer, 1985), although (Fogel et al., 1966) represented another milestone in the evolution of executable structures, through the evolution of finite state machines.

Cramer's goal was to devise a programming language that would be amenable to manipulation by a genetic algorithm and that should produce only well-formed programs (i.e., syntactically correct programs) (Holland, 1975). Described in his work were two approaches: the JB language that adopted an integer list representation, and the TB language that used tree structures. It was found that JB did not satisfy Cramer's second goal of producing only well-formed programs. This was due to the semantic sensitivity of the position of each integer in the list that rendered the representation extremely brittle to change by mutation, and its seeming incompatibility with crossover due to its strong epistatic nature. An example of crossover operators in general can be seen in Figure 2.1. Taking the top example of crossover performed on a string of integers, in the case of the JB language, each integer would represent a program object (e.g. an operator, variable etc.) depending on the integers position. By performing crossover as illustrated it would be possible to produce a syntactically meaningless program, due to the dependencies on the order of previous objects and their semantics. Similarly for mutation, if one of these integers was mutated to another value, it is conceivable that this new value would result in the program being invalid.

TB, which exploited the tree-like structure of its programs, gave rise to the first sub-tree crossover operator for programs. In his concluding remarks, Cramer suggested that bringing the TB representation more in line with the linear nature of the JB representation would allow the exploitation of the power of the binary string genetic algorithm with it's simple genetic operators, or alternatively that it would be possible to extend the TB representation by adopting less standard genetic operators. No evidence exists within the literature of the field to suggest that Cramer followed up on these ideas.

4. TREE-BASED SYSTEMS

Perhaps the most successful, and certainly the most widely adopted representation of computer programs for evolution is the Lisp S-expression, employed by Koza in his seminal paper that was the forerunner for what is now referred to as Genetic Programming (Koza, 1989). This paper stated that string representations had four fundamental problems:

1 They "do not provide the hierarchical structure central to the organization of computer programs (into programs and subroutines)";

2 They "do not provide any convenient way of representing arbitrary computational procedures or incorporating iteration or recursion";

3 They "do not facilitate programs modifying themselves and then executing themselves";

4 That "without dynamic variability, the initial selection of string length limits in advance the number of internal states of the system and the computational complexity of what the system can learn".

Given what had been achieved with linear representations up to that point these statements were correct, but later we will see advances that have allowed linear representations to overcome the problems identified by Koza.

4.1 GENETIC PROGRAMMING

Since its inception, Genetic Programming (GP) has enjoyed much popularity and to date (January 2003) has resulted in the publication of twelve authored books, three edited books, thirteen conference proceedings, over 2,000 papers, its own journal *Genetic Programming and Evolvable Machines* published by Kluwer Academic Publishers, and fifty-eight completed PhD theses (Koza, 2000; Langdon and Koza, 2003).

For a thorough description of GP one should refer to Koza's three books, Genetic Programming 1, 2 and 3 (Koza, 1992; Koza, 1994; Koza et al., 1999), the first GP text book by Banzhaf et al. (Banzhaf et al., 1998), and the Advances in GP series (Kinnear, Jr., 1994; Angeline and Kinnear, Jr., 1996; Spector et al., 1999).

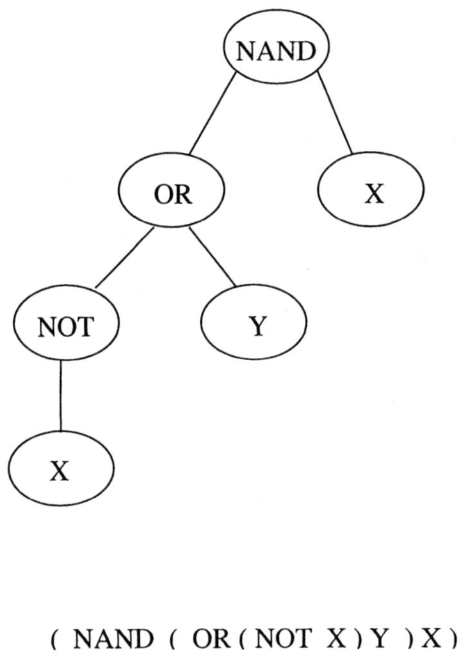

Figure 2.2. An example parse tree of Genetic Programming and the corresponding Lisp S-expression.

The essence of GP is to evolve more complex structures that represent computer programs. The standard version of GP is comprised of a population of Lisp S-expressions represented in the form of parse trees, see Figure 2.2. The parse tree representation facilitates the genetic manipulation of the evolving programs, by using a crossover operator applied to sub-trees, as opposed to solely relying on mutation. In order to evolve a computer program by means of GP, one must specify the primitives of the system, referred to by Koza as the function and terminal sets, before designing a fitness function appropriate to the problem domain. Elements of the terminal set have an arity of zero, that is, they return a numerical or boolean value without taking input values themselves.

An example terminal set, denoted by T, could be as follows:

$$T = \{x, y, z, 1.0\}$$

Note that T contains three variables x, y, and z and a constant 1.0.

The function set, usually denoted as F, is comprised of entities such as operators and functions that usually have an arity greater than zero, that is they can take input values. A function set can contain boolean operators, arithmetic operators, subroutines etc. For example:

$$F = \{NAND, +, -, *, /, moveForward, turnLeft, turnRight\}$$

When choosing primitives one must ensure that the property of *sufficiency* holds, that is, the set of functions and terminals must be able to represent a solution to the problem. One must also ensure that the property of *closure* holds for the function set, that is, each element of the function set must be able to handle all possible input values it may receive, given the total set of primitives available to it and the return values of all other functions. While not essential, it is wise to ensure one's function set is parsimonious, as too large a function set can slow down evolutionary search by needlessly creating a very large search space, as has been demonstrated with GPPS (Koza et al., 1999).

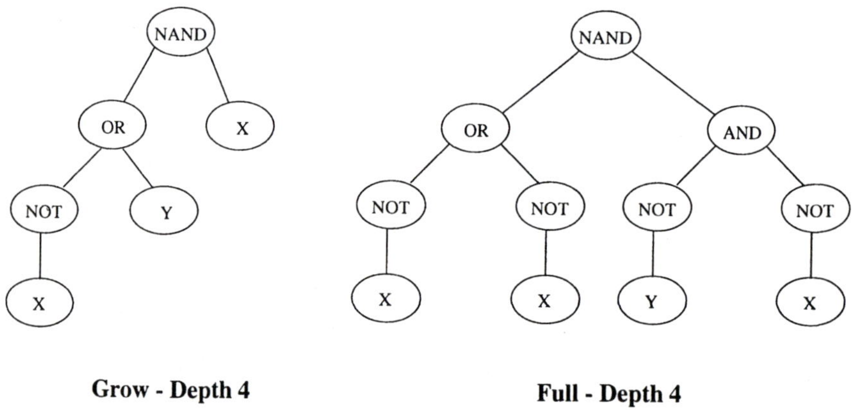

Figure 2.3. The GP individual generation techniques Grow and Full compared for a tree depth of 4.

After selecting the primitives one must specify standard parameters to evolutionary search such as probabilities for genetic operators, population sizes, and selection and replacement mechanisms. In addition, one must specify the maximum tree depths and the type of initialisation method used. Koza outlined the *ramped half-and-half* method for the initialisation of a GP population. The aim of this technique is to facilitate structural diversity in the population, by creating individuals with a uniform distribution of varieties of tree depths. The population is divided equally amongst individuals of a range of tree depths, and then for the number of individuals assigned to a particular depth, half are created using a technique called *grow* and the other half using the *full* technique. With the full technique every tree branch will grow to the full depth allowed resulting in a uniform tree, while the grow technique results in individuals whose branches can be of varying depths up to the maximum depth specified for that group; see Figure 2.3 for examples.

An outline of the standard GP algorithm can be seen in Section 2. This description represents the original version of GP, as outlined by Koza; since then there have been many additions and extensions to tree-based GP, such as the use of ADF's (Koza, 1994), Indexed Memory (Teller, 1994), Strongly typed GP (Montana, 1995), etc.

We will now discuss some of the extensions to tree-based GP, focusing on those approaches whose concepts play a part in the Grammatical Evolution system that is the focus of this book.

4.2 GRAMMAR BASED GENETIC PROGRAMMING

The use of grammars with GP has enjoyed much popularity in recent years. Various approaches have been made using different classes of grammars. Before highlighting the systems that combined grammars with GP we will first give an introduction to grammars, and their standard notation. (Chomsky, 1956) identified a number of different classes of languages and their grammars which he placed in a hierarchy. In increasing complexity these languages are the regular (type 3), context-free (type 2), context-sensitive (type 1), and arbitrary (type 0), where each language is a subclass of the next. In particular, those grammars that are said to be either context-sensitive or context-free are the ones most commonly adopted in GP. These grammars can be represented in Backus Naur Form (Backus et al., 1960; Naur, 1963; Knuth, 1964). The grammars used in GP are typically used in the generative sense to construct a program.

4.2.1 BACKUS NAUR FORM

Backus Naur Form (BNF) is a notation for expressing the grammar of a language in the form of production rules. BNF grammars consist of *terminals*, which are items that can appear in the language, e.g., +, - etc. and *non-terminals*, which can be expanded into one or more terminals and non-terminals. A grammar can be represented by the tuple $\{N, T, P, S\}$, where N is the set of non-terminals, T the set of terminals, P a set of production rules that maps the elements of N to T, and S is a start symbol which is a member of N. When there are a number of productions that can be applied to one element of N the choice is delimited with the '|' symbol. For example,

$$N = \{expr, op, pre - op, var\}$$

$$T = \{sin, cos, +, -, /, *, X, 1.0, (,)\}$$

$$S = expr$$

And P can be represented as:

```
<expr> ::= <expr> <op> <expr>          (a)
         | ( <expr> <op> <expr> )      (b)
         | <pre-op> ( <expr> )         (c)
         | <var>                       (d)

<op> ::= +                             (e)
       | -                             (f)
       | /                             (g)
       | *                             (h)

<pre-op> ::= sin                       (i)
           | cos                       (j)

<var> ::= X                            (k)
        | 1.0                          (l)
```

Unlike the approach in (Koza, 1992), there is no distinction made at this stage between functions (operators in this sense) and terminals (variables in this example); however, this distinction is more of an implementation detail than a design issue. Whigham (Whigham, 1996b) also noted the possible confusion with terminology and used the terms **GPFunctions** and **GPTerminals** for clarity.

In many of the examples to follow, individuals in a population are represented as derivation steps. A derivation step is simply the application of a production rule, P, to an element of the non-terminal set, N. This transformation is denoted by the $\Longrightarrow$ symbol, with the rule being applied written above it.

$$< expr >< op >< expr > \overset{Rule\ (d):\ <expr>::=<var>}{\Longrightarrow} < var >< op >< expr >$$

Above is an example of a derivation step in which we see the application of the rule $Rule\ (d) : < expr > ::=< var >$ to the leftmost non-terminal $< expr >$. This results in $< expr >$ being replaced with $< var >$.

An example of a derivation tree that would comprise an individual of a population in some of the following cases can be seen in Figure 2.4.

This derivation tree can easily be converted into the more familiar parse tree format adopted by tree-based GP, see Figure 2.5. It is more difficult, however, to convert a parse tree into an equivalent derivation tree, as the process is usually non-deterministic.

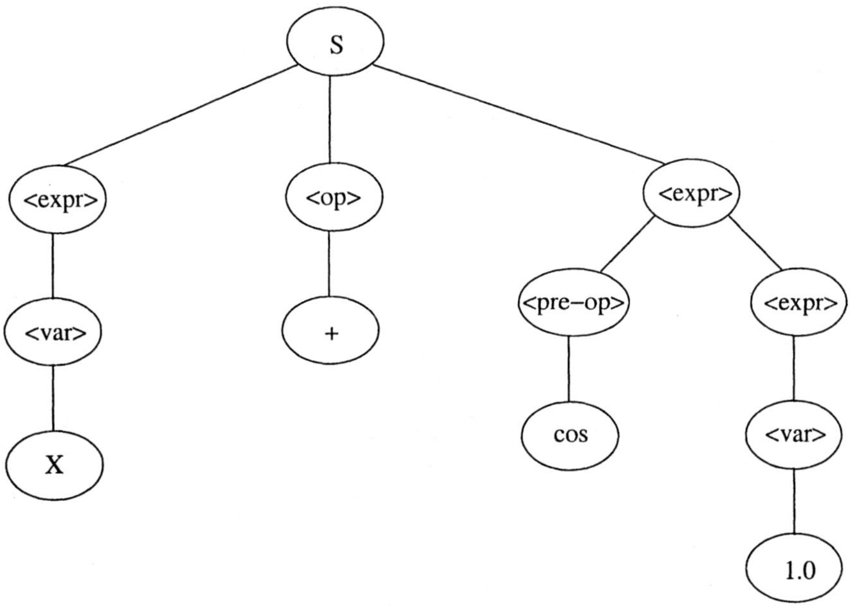

Figure 2.4. An example of a derivation tree for a grammar-based GP individual.

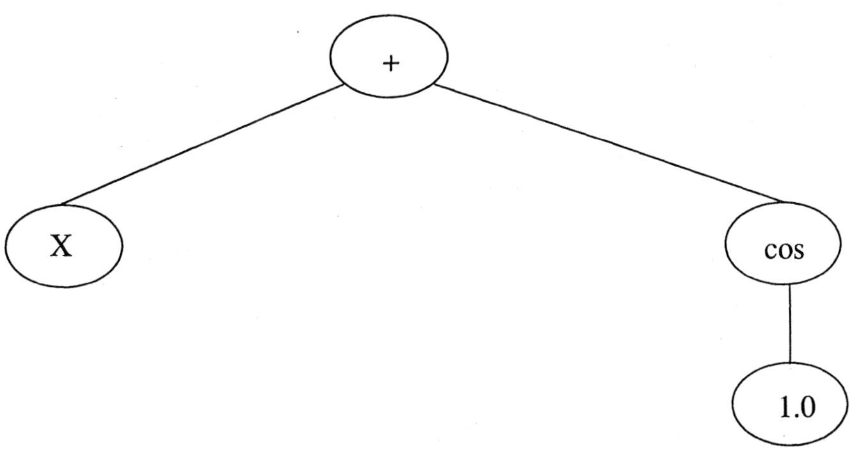

Figure 2.5. The example derivation tree of Figure 2.4 converted into its equivalent parse tree.

4.2.2 CELLULAR ENCODING

Gruau describes an approach that enables the representation of neural networks in the form of trees, which made it possible to manipulate them by GP (Gruau, 1994). The approach represents neural networks in the form of cellular encoding, which in turn is represented in the form of a graph grammar. This is used to generate the trees of the GP population.

A graph grammar represents a set of rules for re-writing the topology of a graph. This is an embryonic approach to the generation of the neural networks, where each cell of the neural network corresponds to a node of the graph being constructed by the grammar. Starting from an ancestor cell, rules of the graph grammar are applied to cells, resulting in the division of the ancestor cell into further cells with properties that may differ from those of the original cell. The final result is a complete neural network where the evolutionary process alone determines its size and functionality. Koza et al. have adopted a similar embryonic approach to the evolution of analog circuits (Koza et al., 1999).

4.2.3 BIAS IN GP

The work of Whigham represents an application of grammars to tree-based GP as a means to incorporate declarative and learnt bias (Whigham, 1996a; Whigham, 1995a). Declarative bias is the representation of knowledge separate from the learning system, and is provided by the initial grammar given to the system. Over the evolutionary search it is possible to incorporate changes into the grammar and this is what constitutes the learnt bias. Bias, in the form of the context-free grammar, is used in the creation of the initial population to narrow the possible representations that the system may adopt. The grammar is also used during the application of the genetic operators to ensure the syntactic correctness of individuals.

4.2.4 GENETIC PROGRAMMING KERNEL

Independently of Whigham, Geyer-Schulz developed a similar derivation tree representation (Geyer-Schulz, 1995), that was later implemented by Horner as the Genetic Programming Kernel (GPK) (Horner, 1996; Geyer-Schulz, 1997).

The GPK has been criticised (Paterson and Livesey, 1997) for the difficulty associated with creating the first generation - considerable effort must be put into ensuring that all the trees represent valid sequences, and that none grow without bounds.

4.2.5 COMBINING GP AND ILP

Wong and Leung describe an approach that employs logic grammars with tree-based GP, referred to as LOGENPRO (LOgic grammars based GENetic PROgramming system) (Wong and Leung, 1994; Wong, 1995; Wong and Leung, 1997). Billed as being a framework to combine GP and Inductive Logic Programming (ILP), LOGENPRO has enjoyed much success in its application to the area of data mining (Wong and Leung, 2000). Derivation trees, as in Figure 2.4, are the representation of choice for individuals in the population. Logic grammars differ from standard context-free grammars in that both the terminals as well as the non-terminals can include arguments. Arguments in the grammar can be used to force context-dependency, thus the logic grammar is a member of the class of context-sensitive grammars. The arguments can also be used to generate tree structures in the course of parsing which in turn can be used to infer semantics of the program.

4.2.6 AUTO-PARALLELISATION WITH GP

One interesting application/variation of tree-based GP has been its use in the area of auto-parallelisation of serial code. A transformational approach is adopted in a manner not dissimilar to that of Gruau (Gruau, 1994). The essence is to transform a functionally correct serial program into a functionally equivalent parallel version. Each individual in the population is a set of transformations that are used to carry out the process of parallelisation, and so the best set of transformations is evolved.

Note, however, that this approach does not use grammars. There have been numerous publications on this subject (Ryan and Walsh, 1997; Ryan and Ivan, 1999; Ryan, 1999).

5. STRING BASED GP

In parallel to developments with tree-based GP, major advances have been made with the use of string based Evolutionary Automatic Programming systems. One of the major reasons for the continuation of research in this area is the potential benefits that can arise from a separation of the genotype and phenotype that does not exist in tree-based systems. In GP, evolution is generally conducted upon the actual programs that are the product of the process (the phenotype). If we were to allow evolution to be conducted upon another representation of the program (the genotype) it must be mapped onto a functional program (phenotype). A full discussion on this is deferred until chapter 3.

Many of the advances made in linear systems have been accompanied by the adoption of grammars for much the same reasons as those in tree-based GP systems, that is, to ensure the syntactic correctness of evolving programs. As Grammatical Evolution adopts grammars we will focus in particular on those linear systems that use grammars to some degree.

5.1 BGP

Banzhaf (Banzhaf, 1994) and later (Keller and Banzhaf, 1996) described a linear GP system that employed a genotype-phenotype mapping from a linear genotype into a linear phenotype, using a context free programming language. The system, referred to as Binary Genetic Programming (BGP), adopts a context-free grammar for a repair procedure during the mapping from the linear genome to the output language.

The genotype in this case is a binary string that contains *codons* of a predetermined number of bits, each of which represents a symbol of the output language. The mapping of codon to symbol is explicitly determined at the outset. In a manner similar to the biological code, they adopt a redundant genetic code, that is, many different codons can represent the same language symbol. An example of such a mapping can be seen in Figure 2.6.

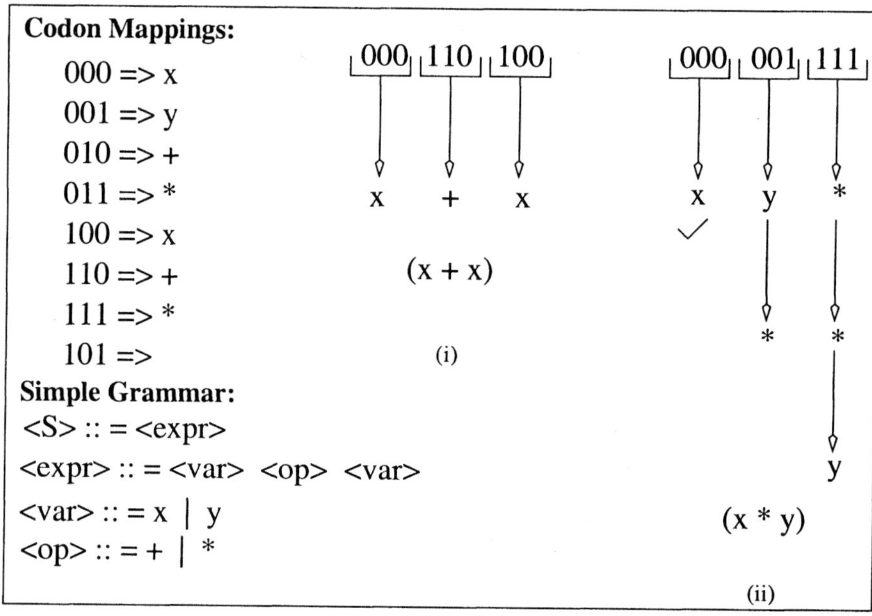

Figure 2.6. Example 3 bit codon codes with their corresponding symbols for Binary Genetic Programming. Note redundancy in the mapping. (i) Illustrates a straightforward mapping from codons to a valid expression $x + x$. (ii) Demonstrates the repair mechanism, where the second symbol y is illegal in this position and must be replaced with a legal symbol according to a grammar. In this case valid symbols for this position could be $*$ or $+$. y is replaced with the symbol whose codon has the closest hamming distance (bit flips), i.e. $*$. The third original symbol, $*$, is now illegal and so the repair mechanism is employed resulting in it being replaced with y.

Their experiments suggest benefits, in terms of improvement in performance (higher fitness), in adopting a genotype-phenotype mapping over standard genetic programming and that further analysis of the genetic codes was required. It was not clear as to what, if any, effect the redundancy in the genetic code was playing in the success of this system. Later (Keller and Banzhaf, 1999) an investigation was conducted in which it was possible to evolve the genetic code itself. It was found that the code tended towards redundancy for certain symbols, that is, evolution was able to learn the significance of those symbols for the problem being addressed. The ability to evolve the genetic code during the evolutionary search has the potential to enhance the ability to solve dynamic problems, as changes in the genetic code could enable the search process to keep up with the changing topology of the search landscape. The authors suggest that the ability to evolve the genetic code could be of particular use in data mining applications where the functional relation between variables are unknown, and as such could enhance the learning of significant functional relations (Keller and Banzhaf, 2001).

5.2 MACHINE CODE GENETIC PROGRAMMING

A machine code, linear GP system originally called the Compiling Genetic Programming system, now AIM-GP(Automatic Induction of Machine Code for Genetic Programming), has been developed that is up to 1000 times faster than a standard GP system (Nordin, 1994; Nordin and Banzhaf, 1995b; Francone et al., 1996; Nordin, 1997; Nordin, 1998; Nordin et al., 1999). A commercial version of AIM-GP has been recently released under the name of Discipulus^{TM} (RML Technologies, 1998).

AIM-GP adopts a linear binary string genome to maximise efficiency gains, as it means the individuals (machine code programs) can be directly evaluated on the hardware architecture of the machine without having to undergo either a mapping or interpretation stage. Like a standard tree-based GP system, evolution acts directly upon the program with no genotype-phenotype distinction. Results on various classification problems have shown that CGP's performance is comparable to other Machine Learning paradigms, such as classifier systems, and multilayer feedforward neural networks.

Each individual in AIM-GP is a machine code function comprised of four parts, a header and footer, the main function body itself containing many instruction blocks, and a return statement (see Figure 2.7). Evolution is directed towards the 32-bit instruction blocks of the function's body, each of which can contain one or more instructions of 8, 16, 24 or 32 bits with a combined size of 32-bits. The genetic operator of crossover is restricted to the boundaries of the instruction blocks, and mutation acts by either randomly generating a new instruction block, or by randomly changing an operand or operator of one of the instructions. Two variants of crossover are adopted, a standard two-point,

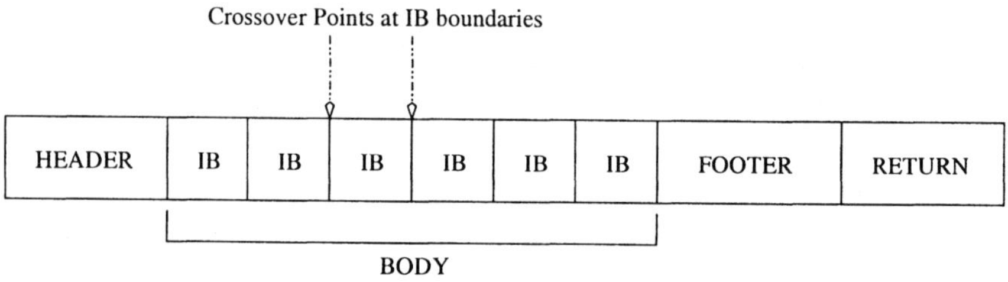

Figure 2.7. An AIM-GP individual is a machine code function comprised of a header, a body containing one or more 32-bit instruction blocks (IB's), a footer and a return block.

and a homologous crossover that swaps instruction blocks located at the same locus (Francone et al., 1999).

5.3 GENETIC ALGORITHM FOR DERIVING SOFTWARE

Paterson & Livesley described a Genetic Algorithm (GA) approach to the automatic generation of programs called the Genetic Algorithm for Deriving Software (GADS) (Paterson and Livesey, 1996; Paterson and Livesey, 1997). Like Binary Genetic Programming, described in Section 5.1, fixed-length, binary, linear genomes are employed with a genotype-phenotype mapping process to generate programs, but BNF Grammars are utilised in GADS as the output language specification. The BNF of GADS is extended to include a default symbol for each non-terminal of the grammar. The default symbols are used if the situation arises where all the genes of an individual have been read during the mapping process and the mapping is incomplete, that is, elements of the non-terminal set still appear in the expression being mapped. The default rules are then applied in order to complete the mapping process.

During the mapping from genotype to phenotype, a parse tree is generated, by initialising the root node to the start symbol of the grammar. Starting from the left-most gene, the integer value of each gene is read, and, if the value corresponds to a suitable production rule, that rule is applied to the current non-terminal. If the gene value does not correspond to an appropriate rule the gene is skipped and another read. The mapping process terminates upon reaching the end of the individual's chromosome, at which point any remaining non-terminals are replaced with their default symbols. Paterson & Livesley concede that a weakness in this approach lies in the fact that given large grammars, the likelihood of any one particular production rule being selected is diminished. In order to improve the chances of specific rules being selected, rule weighting, achieved by the duplication of some productions in the grammar to promote their use, was adopted. Paterson also employed the strategies of increasing population sizes and increasing individual lengths as a measure to counteract this problem. Another potential weakness of this approach is the manner in which genes are skipped if unsuitable for the current non-terminal. This often results in a proliferation of introns that can choke effective evolutionary search, and can also leave the system open to a reliance on the user-defined default terminals. As one does not always know what would be the ideal terminal in every situation for each non-terminal in the grammar, it would be a more desirable approach to let evolution decide what terminals are adopted.

5.4 CFG/GP

Freeman describes an approach called Context Free Grammars GP (CFG/GP) that is very similar to GADS (Freeman, 1998). Again, fixed length linear genomes are employed where genes are integer values. There is a subtle difference during the mapping process that distinguishes it from GADS; instead of attempting to apply rules specified by each gene to the next non-terminal (left-most), each gene is read and can be applied to any suitable non-terminal in the partially mapped parse tree. Given the similarity to GADS, this system suffers from similar drawbacks in terms of scalability of the grammar and the likelihood of specifying any one rule, the proliferation of introns although not necessarily to the same extent given the subtle difference in approach during the mapping from genotype to phenotype, and the use of pre-determined default rules.

6. CONCLUSIONS

The above is by no means an exhaustive representation of all the approaches adopted in Evolutionary Automatic Programming [2], it is rather a sample of those systems of particular importance and relevance to the subject of this book, that is, Evolutionary Automatic Programming in an arbitrary language. Without some of the developments outlined above it would not have been possible to arrive at the Grammatical Evolution system; we owe much inspiration to those whose work has gone before us. Before detailing the Grammatical Evolution system in chapter 4, we will discuss what we consider to be the fundamental characteristics of an Evolutionary Automatic Programming system, by paying particular attention to lessons that can be learned from Molecular Biology.

[2] For example, two other recent techniques that could be considered Evolutionary Automatic Programming are Probabilistic Incremental Program Evolution (PIPE) (Salustowicz and Schmidhuber, 1997) and the Automatic Design of Algorithms through Evolution (ADATE) (Olsson, 1994; Olsson, 1995; Olsson, 1999).

Chapter 3

LESSONS FROM MOLECULAR BIOLOGY

1. INTRODUCTION

This chapter discusses some of the fundamental principles from Molecular Biology that can be exploited by an Evolutionary Automatic Programming system. In particular, we focus on those aspects that have provided inspiration for Grammatical Evolution. We will see later in chapter 4 how some of these principles have been adopted successfully by the Grammatical Evolution system.

In recent years, there has been an increase in the body of research conducted on gene expression in evolutionary computation. Notable areas include genotype-phenotype distinction (Ryan et al., 1998; Banzhaf, 1994; Gruau, 1994), genetic-code evolution (Keller and Banzhaf, 1999; Keller and Banzhaf, 2001), distributed fitness evaluation (Kargupta and Sarkar, 1999), diploidy (Collins and Ryan, 1999; Goldberg, 1987; Hollstein, 1971; Ng and Wong, 1995; Ošmera et al., 1997), polygenic inheritance (Ryan and Collins, 1998), role of introns (Kargupta, 1997), degenerate genetic codes and neutral mutations (O'Neill and Ryan, 1999b; Barreau, 2000; Barnett, 1997; Banzhaf, 1994; Vassilev and Miller, 2000).

In the context of Evolutionary Automatic Programming, a distinction of genotype and phenotype is perhaps the most powerful area that can be exploited. Virtually all life forms on this planet employ this distinction, and we show in section 5 some of the beneficial properties that can be derived from its use. Arising from a genotype-phenotype distinction, issues such as the role of the genetic code and gene expression play increasing importance. Before discussing the potential benefits that can be obtained from these in Evolutionary Automatic Programming, however, we will firstly discuss the genetic code and gene expression models of biological systems as determined through research

Table 3.1. The Genetic Code of biological organisms. The full names for the amino acids are given in Table 3.2. Notice the redundancy that occurs for most of the 20 naturally occurring amino acids. In general, this code can be considered universal across most species, although variations do arise.

	U	C	A	G	
U	UUU - Phe	UCU - Ser	UAU - Tyr	UGU - Cys	U
	UUC - Phe	UCC - Ser	UAC - Tyr	UGC - Cys	C
	UUA - Leu	UCA - Ser	UAA - Stop	UGA - Stop	A
	UUG - Leu	UCG - Ser	UAG - Stop	UGG - Trp	G
C	CUU - Leu	CCU - Pro	CAU - His	CGU - Arg	U
	CUC - Leu	CCC - Pro	CAC - His	CGC - Arg	C
	CUA - Leu	CCA - Pro	CAA - Gln	CGA - Arg	A
	CUG - Leu	CCG - Pro	CAG - Gln	CGG - Arg	G
A	AUU - Ile	ACU - Thr	AAU - Asn	AGU - Ser	U
	AUC - Ile	ACC - Thr	AAC - Asn	AGC - Ser	C
	AUA - Ile	ACA - Thr	AAA - Lys	AGA - Arg	A
	AUG - Met	ACG - Thr	AAG - Lys	AGG - Arg	G
G	GUU - Val	GCU - Ala	GAU - Asp	GGU - Gly	U
	GUC - Val	GCC - Ala	GAC - Asp	GGC - Gly	C
	GUA - Val	GCA - Ala	GAA - Glu	GGA - Gly	A
	GUG - Val	GCG - Ala	GAG - Glu	GGG - Gly	G

in the field of Molecular Biology. This will be followed by a discussion on the neutral theory of evolution and the possible benefits this phenomenon can bring to evolutionary computation.

2. GENETIC CODES & GENE EXPRESSION MODELS

Molecular Biology, a relatively young scientific field, has yielded many insights into the innermost workings of the fundamental units of complex organisms, the cell. Discoveries include the structure of the hereditary material deoxyribonucleic acid (DNA), the discovery of proteins and their structural units, the elucidation of the genetic code, and the complex signalling networks that exist within and between cells. Of utmost importance is what has become known as *the central dogma of Molecular Biology*. This tenet describes the processes of transcription and translation, i.e., that DNA is transcribed to messenger ribonucleic acid (mRNA), which in turn is translated into protein. Proteins are responsible for the generation of phenotypic traits, such as eye colour, and height.

DNA contains the genetic code that specifies the constituent units of proteins, called amino acids. Each amino acid, and their sequences within a protein, is represented by a particular sequence of the molecules that make up the genetic

Table 3.2. The three letter amino acid codes as in Tables 3.1 with their corresponding full amino acid names.

Code	Name	Code	Name
Phe	Phenylalanine	**Leu**	Leucine
Tyr	Tyrosine	**Cys**	Cysteine
Trp	Tryptophan	**Pro**	Proline
His	Histidine	**Gln**	Glutamine
Arg	Arginine	**Ile**	Isoleucine
Met	Methionine	**Thr**	Threonine
Asn	Asparagine	**Lys**	Lysine
Ser	Serine	**Val**	Valine
Ala	Alanine	**Asp**	Aspartic Acid
Glu	Glutamic Acid	**Gly**	Glycine

code. Specifically, groups of three molecules, called bases, code for a single amino acid. A group of three bases is referred to as a codon.
A base is one of the molecules Adenine (A), Thymine (T), Guanine (G), and Cytosine (C) in DNA, and Uracil (U) instead of Thymine in RNA.

Table 3.1 outlines the complete human genetic code for both DNA and RNA. Proteins are generated during the process of translation that literally translates the base triplets into their corresponding amino acids. There are 20 naturally occurring amino acids and 64 triplet sequences, called codons. Three of these codons are used to specify the termination of translation and do not generally specify amino acids. This means that there are 61 codons to code for the 20 naturally occurring amino acids. As a result the genetic code is degenerate, that is, there is a many-to-one mapping such that an amino acid can be specified by many different codons. This occurs through a phenomenon known as the *wobble hypothesis* (Crick, 1966), and it means that a mutation at the third position in a codon does not always result in the code for a different amino acid.

Such mutations are referred to as *silent* or *neutral* mutations, and these have possible implications for evolutionary search and dynamics (Kimura, 1983).

There has been some work recently on the evolutionary consequences of degeneracy[1] (referred to as redundancy in previous work in the evolutionary computation community) in natural and artificial genetic codes (O'Neill and Ryan, 1999b; Barreau, 2000; Vassilev and Miller, 2000). The major conse-

[1] We recommend the adoption of the term genetic code degeneracy as this is the terminology used in Molecular Biology, and is a more correct description of the phenomenon. Redundancy is usually used in the context of genetic material surplus to requirement in the field of evolutionary computation e.g. introns. As such, we feel it is important to draw the distinction between these two subtly different but related phenomena.

quences of neutral evolution and degenerate genetic codes for evolutionary computation are discussed in Section 3, which follows.

Ongoing areas of investigation are the regulatory processes that exist to control the expression of particular proteins from specific genes along the DNA in different organisms. The discovery of special regions along the DNA yielded the formation of the operon model (Jacob and Monod, 1961). These regions, known as repressors, promoters, and operators are involved in the regulation of the expression of specific genes, e.g. the prokaryotic lac operon that contains three genes associated with the metabolism of lactose[2]. An overview of the operon model can be seen in Figure 3.1.

What is crucial to note when dealing with gene expression is that it occurs within a cellular environment with complex feedback loops controlling the further expression of genes. While all cells in an organism have identical genetic material, each cell has the ability to specialise in terms of functionality and structure, depending on what genes are expressed at certain stages of cell development. In (Kennedy, 1998) a novel artificial model of a biological cell is presented in which each cell has a genome and metabolism. Pairs of these genomes and metabolisms co-evolve using a genetic algorithm. A simple genomic language is introduced that follows Jacob and Monod's operon model (Jacob and Monod, 1961), such that genes can be placed at any loci on the genome. Thus, a model is generated in which the genome specifies proteins such as enzymes that can catalyse metabolic reactions, and the chemicals of metabolism have the ability to regulate genes and allow expression of proteins from the genome. The model, partly Lamarckian due to the manner in which the metabolism evolves, is found to be more efficient at solving the boot-strapping problem due to the co-evolution of the metabolism with the genome. The boot-strapping problem involves finding genomes and metabolisms that can work together in a synergistic fashion to result in stable cells for a target environment.

3. NEUTRAL THEORY OF EVOLUTION

A recent upsurgence of interest in the role of selectively neutral evolution in evolutionary dynamics has brought about the concepts of *neutral mutations* and *neutral networks*. A neutral mutation is a mutation event, typically a point mutation that has no effect upon the phenotypic fitness of an individual in a population. The term neutral network has been coined to describe a group of individuals that are connected by neutral mutations.

[2]The lac operon of the prokaryotic bacteria E. coli contains 3 genes that enable the organism to metabolise the disaccharide lactose. The genes of the lac operon enable the breakdown of lactose into glucose which is critical to the survival of the bacteria as it is used in energy production amongst numerous other functions.

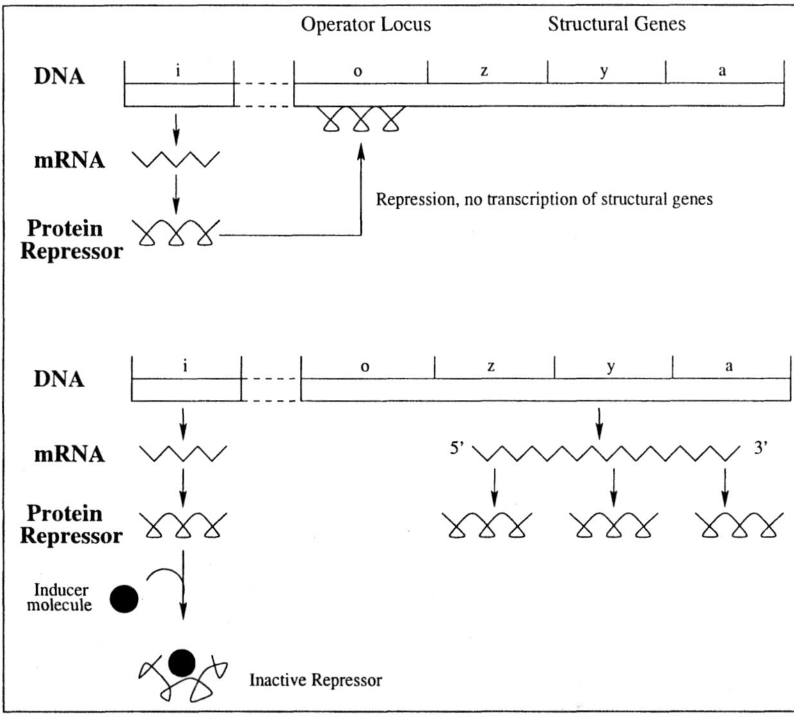

Figure 3.1. A diagram illustrating a modified form of the operon model as described by Jacob and Monod (*i* was thought to be an mRNA rather than a protein). The *i* gene encodes a repressor that binds tightly to the operator *o* locus, thereby preventing transcription of the mRNA from the *z*, *y*, and *a* structural genes. When inducer is present, it combines with repressor, changing its structure so it can no longer bind to the operator locus, thus allowing translation of the three structural genes. The inducer also has the ability to remove repressor already complexed with the *o* locus.

Kimura was perhaps the first to recognise the potential neutral mutations have to effect evolution (Kimura, 1983). He devised the neutral theory of molecular evolution, which stated that most of evolution occurs via mutations that are neutral with respect to selection, and thus evolution occurs via the resulting random genetic drift. An interesting observation arising from this is that given a continuous variation of genetic material, one would have a mechanism to explain the occurrence of genetic diversity within natural populations. In the field of Genetic Programming, Banzhaf took neutral theory into account when employing a genotype to phenotype mapping. This enables the generation of genetic diversity within his artificial populations allowing his algorithm to escape local optima (Banzhaf, 1994). The ability for neutral mutations to occur in Banzhaf's algorithm arose due to the use of a hand coded degenerate genetic code.

EA practitioners often adopt the notion of *fitness landscapes*, as do biologists. These fitness landscapes can help us to visualise evolutionary dynamics so one could say, for example, that selection acts as a force driving a population up a fitness peak, while mutations serve to disperse the population, counteracting to some extent the selective force. One problem for the evolutionary computation community is the problem of a population becoming trapped on a local optimum due to selective pressure. Given that in biological populations this does not appear to be the case, this suggests that a piece(s) of the puzzle is missing and, as such, our models of evolutionary dynamics over these fitness landscapes would appear to be incomplete. For example, in (van Nimwegen and Crutchfield, 1999) evidence has been presented to suggest that a population undergoing evolution on a fitness landscape with neutrality tends to concentrate itself at highly connected regions of the neutral networks. This allows mutation to occur, changing the genotypic sequence, while ensuring preservation of the functionality.

Work by Kimura, Eigen and others on RNA evolution suggests that the existence of neutral networks gives a different perspective on evolutionary dynamics over a fitness landscape (Eigen et al., 1989; Huynen, 1995; Huynen et al., 1996; Erik van Nimwegen, 1999; van Nimwegen and Crutchfield, 1999; Reidys, 1995; Reidys et al., 1997; Reidys et al., 1998). Rather than the traditional view of a population performing hill climbing, we now have the scenario where a population could also be drifting along these neutral networks with the occasional jump between adjacent networks. Of particular significance is when these networks are said to *percolate* a landscape, that is to say, they are arbitrarily close to every other neutral network, then, given time, almost any possible fitness can be attained by the population. Artificial system simulations of the evolution of molecular species (Newman and Engelhardt, 1998; Engelhardt, 1998) state the claim that the fitness attainable during evolution on a fitness landscape with neutrality increases with increasing degrees of neutrality, and is also directly related to the fitness of the most fit percolating network. This finding could prove to be beneficial to those problems of a dynamic nature or where an ideal fitness is difficult to define or unknown.

4. FURTHER PRINCIPLES

As well as those principles outlined above there are countless additional biological concepts that can be introduced into our algorithms, we do not attempt to catalogue them here, however, many examples may already be found in the literature. Examples include, novel genetic search operators such as homologous crossover (Francone et al., 1999; Langdon, 2000), self-adapting algorithms (e.g., evolution of genetic code (Keller and Banzhaf, 1999), mutation rates and population sizes (Sheehan, 2000; Goldberg et al., 1991a) etc.), polygenic inheritance (Ryan, 1996), and epigenetic inheritance (Paton, 1994). In addition, (Paton, 1997) and (De Jong, 1999) identify a number of areas that are open to investigation.

In the next section we will present potential advantages to be gained by incorporating principles from Molecular Biology, discussed up to this point, into our algorithms.

5. DESIRABLE FEATURES

We will now outline some of the desirable features that an Evolutionary Automatic Programming system might gain with the incorporation of the previously discussed principles from Molecular Biology.

1 Generalised encoding that can represent a variety of structures, similar to how DNA codes for a variety of proteins.

2 Efficiency gains for evolutionary search, by taking advantage of neutral evolution.

3 Maintenance of genetic diversity within an evolving population through a degenerate encoding.

4 Preservation of functionality while allowing continuation of search also with the adoption of a degenerate encoding.

5 Re-use of genetic material as a result of gene expression.

6 A compression of representation through re-use of genetic material.

7 Alternative implementation of functions with the introduction of gene expression control mechanisms in the spirit of operons.

8 Positional Independence as observed through the meaning of DNA/RNA bases and amino acids from proteins being preserved independently of their molecular context.

The first feature, a generalised encoding that can represent a variety of structures, is the main advantage for Evolutionary Automatic Programming. This could be achieved with an abstraction of our genotype from the output program, thus allowing a mapping process that can be utilised to generate code in an arbitrary language.

In order to achieve efficiency gains for the evolutionary search, the second feature above, the adoption of a degenerate genetic code could prove useful. If the output program is not directly represented within the genotype, as would be the case if our first feature was implemented, it would be possible to adopt a degenerate code. This can lead to efficiency gains through the use of neutral mutations and their corresponding neutral networks, see (Barnett, 1997; Newman and Engelhardt, 1998). A degenerate code exists when many different codes are in existence that corresponds to the same phenotypic symbol. Given findings in (Newman and Engelhardt, 1998) that given a higher degree of neutrality greater fitness' can be attainable, it would be interesting to incorporate a genetic code with a tuneable degree of neutrality.

As found in (Banzhaf, 1994) and suggested by (Kimura, 1983) a degenerate code can also facilitate genetic diversity, the third of the features we have outlined above. This genetic diversity could be maintained during runs through the distinction of genotype and phenotype. Maintenance of genetic diversity is of particular importance in the field of evolutionary computation to overcome the problem of premature convergence. A population is said to have converged if it has become stuck on a local optimum with no means of freeing itself. There can be no further evolution in this case and unless the local optimum happens to correspond to the global optimum the evolutionary search has failed. For a discussion on strategies to prevent premature convergence refer to (Ryan, 1996).

Evolutionary search can be facilitated by enabling the preservation of functionality (fourth feature), thus allowing individuals to survive due to their phenotypic fitness while still allowing variations in their genotype. This effect can be facilitated when a genotype-phenotype distinction exists with the presence of a many-to-one mapping from genotype to phenotype. One example of this occurring is when evolutionary search is moving along a neutral network as discussed earlier. The mapping process can also either incorporate some form of a repair mechanism or inherently have the ability to ensure that no matter what happens to the genotype a valid phenotype will always be generated. Refer to (Yu and Bentley, 1998) for a discussion on generating legal phenotypes from a genotype.

The fifth feature, the re-use of genetic material, can be achieved with ease when a genotype-phenotype distinction is present. The same genetic material can be used during any one mapping from genotype to phenotype. In chapter 2, examples of linear GP systems were given where, when the end of the genotype is reached during mapping and the individual concerned has not yet been fully mapped, that some pre-determined default symbols were substituted where gaps existed. Having the possibility of gene expression at hand it would be possible to re-use some or all of the genetic material in order to attempt a completion of the mapping process. We subscribe to the notion that it is preferable to let the evolutionary process decide what to do in these cases, rather than settling for pre-determined values.

Given the existence of the fifth feature, it would be possible to attain the sixth feature of a compression of representation. That is, in terms of programs, large structures can be represented with a relatively small genotype. Such a scenario could arise through a mechanism like gene overlapping. In biology this can occur in two distinct ways each of which could arise, that is, either through a simple re-use of genetic material or by alternative reading frames. In the first instance a fragment of a gene may also code for another shorter protein and is simply reused. The second instance is slightly more complex, in that the same genotype region may code for completely different proteins by simply changing the reading frame at the transcription level, see Figure 3.2. That is, instead of starting transcription from the first nucleotide of a sequence, the process commences from the second or third nucleotide positions, with the result that different codons, and therefore, different amino acids are produced than when transcription began at the first nucleotide position.

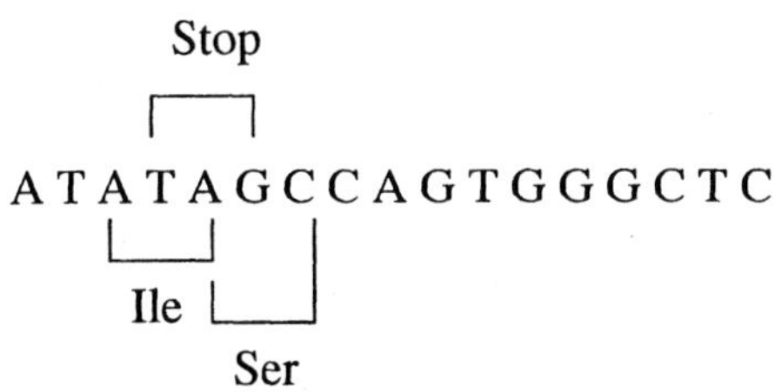

Figure 3.2. An illustration of alternative reading frames for a DNA nucleotide sequence fragment. Depending on which nucleotide the transcription process commences from a different amino acid product results. The ATA codon corresponds to the amino acid Isoleucine (Ile), TAG is a Stop codon denoting the end of a gene, and AGC codes the amino acid Serine (Ser).

Through the implementation of transcription level control over gene expression it could be possible to introduce the seventh feature, whereby different regions of the genome could behave in a manner similar to functions in genetic programming. That is, a gene located at one locus might invoke the expression of another gene from a different locus, thus allowing modularisation of functionality. The operon model discussed earlier could be considered as a natural example of such a setup. Note in this case, a feedback loop is necessary from phenotype to genotype to allow such a regulatory mechanism to exist, i.e., that the phenotype can effect the manner in which transcription can occur.

The eighth feature, positional independence, amounts to the position (locus) of a gene on the chromosome bearing no effect on its functionality. For example, this useful phenomenon could also be achieved using the operon model, or some alternative gene expression mechanism, by allowing metabolites to recognise a specific promoter region on the chromosome, thus switching on or off that particular gene (or set of genes) expression. Alternatively, this could be achieved through novel genetic codings at the translation step. In terms of Evolutionary Automatic Programming, positional independence could give rise to more productive crossover events due to the separation of locus and function.

6. CONCLUSIONS

We have identified some of the benefits that could be made available to an Evolutionary Automatic Programming system that adopts the principles from Molecular Biology outlined in this chapter. Most of the benefits that can arise are due to a genotype-phenotype distinction. In the following chapter we will show how many of the advantages outlined above are incorporated into the Grammatical Evolution system. In subsequent chapters we will report on an analysis of some of these features as they appear in Grammatical Evolution and demonstrate how they contribute to its success.

Chapter 4

GRAMMATICAL EVOLUTION

1. INTRODUCTION

This chapter describes Grammatical Evolution (GE) in detail (Ryan et al., 1998; O'Neill and Ryan, 2001; O'Neill, 2001). We show that it is an evolutionary algorithm (EA) that can evolve complete programs in an arbitrary language using a variable-length binary string. The binary genome determines which production rules in a Backus Naur Form (BNF) grammar definition are used in a genotype-to-phenotype mapping process to a program. GE is set up such that the evolutionary algorithm is independent of the output programs by virtue of the genotype-phenotype mapping, allowing GE to take advantage of advances in EA research. The BNF grammar, like the EA, is a plug-in component of the system that determines the syntax and language of the output code, hence, it is possible to evolve programs in an arbitrary language.

EAs have been used with much success for the automatic generation of programs. In particular, genetic programming (GP) has enjoyed considerable popularity and widespread use (Koza, 1992; Koza, 1994; Koza et al., 1999).

GP originally employed Lisp as its target language, however, many experimenters generate a home grown language, specific to their particular problem.

GE does not perform the evolutionary process on the actual programs, but rather on variable-length binary strings. A mapping process is employed to generate programs in any language by using the binary strings to select production rules in a Backus Naur Form (BNF) grammar definition. The result is the construction of a syntactically correct program from a binary string that can then be evaluated by a fitness function.

We have named this approach Grammatical Evolution to avoid any confusion with traditional GP, that is, GE adopts a genotype-phenotype distinction and explicitly uses grammars to generate the output programs. As stated earlier in chapter 2, we recommend that a better description for both of these approaches is Evolutionary Automatic Programming due to the differences between the various types of GP described previously.

As noted in (Banzhaf, 1994; Keller and Banzhaf, 1996) and chapter 3, a mapping process and its subsequent separation of search and solution spaces can result in benefits such as the unconstrained search of the genotype while still ensuring validity/legality of the program's output. For a discussion on various methods of generating legal phenotypes from a genotype see (Yu and Bentley, 1998). Another potential benefit of such a morphogenic process is that genetic diversity may be enhanced based on the neutral theory of evolution (Kimura, 1983), which states that most mutations driving the evolutionary process are neutral with respect to the phenotype; that is, a mutation may have no effect on the phenotypic fitness of an individual. See chapter 3 for a more detailed discussion. This phenomenon is facilitated in this system by the use of a degenerate genetic code that is observed in biological genetic systems. This degenerate code facilitates the occurrence of neutral mutations, a consequence of which is that various genotypes can represent the same phenotype, thus facilitating the maintenance of genetic diversity within a population.

2. BACKGROUND

GE is not the first instance in which grammars have been used with evolutionary approaches to automatic programming. A number of other attempts using grammars with GP have been made (Keller and Banzhaf, 1996; Whigham, 1995a; Wong and Leung, 1995; Gruau, 1994; Horner, 1996; Paterson and Livesey, 1997; Freeman, 1998), largely to overcome the so-called "closure" problem, the generation and preservation of valid programs. A more detailed discussion on this area can be found in chapter 2, Section 2.4.2. As well as examining the closure problem, Whigham (Whigham, 1995a) used grammars as a method to introduce bias into the evolutionary process (Whigham, 1995b; Whigham, 1996b). The grammar is used to introduce declarative bias by specifying all the legal statements that can be generated. The grammar could therefore be used to incorporate knowledge by specifying the structure that a solution might take, for example, whether it is multiline with conditional statements and loops or simply a single line of code. Grammars were also allowed to be modified during runs, thus allowing the system to modify the bias initially specified.

As in Wong and Leung (Wong and Leung, 1995), and Horner (Horner, 1996), derivation trees are used as the genotype representation by Whigham. The derivation trees state exactly which production rules are to be used at any time during the mapping process onto the phenotype. In (Horner, 1996), an implementation of a grammar based GP system is described in which a great deal of effort is put into generating complete derivation trees for the initial generation to ensure the individuals are complete programs and to ensure variation in the size and shapes of solutions. As with all tree-based GP systems, the genetic operators must be designed to maintain closure of the generated programs. Wong and Leung adopted logic grammars, a member of the class of context-sensitive grammars, in which both the terminals and non-terminals can include arguments, thus allowing context-dependency to be enforced.

Paterson & Livesley (Paterson and Livesey, 1997) and later Freeman (Freeman, 1998) attempted to overcome the problem of generating the initial generation by introducing a repair mechanism that used default values in the case that a non-terminal was left without a terminal having been specified. Each uses fixed-length integer arrays as the genotype representation, where each integer represents a production rule from the BNF. When rules cannot be applied in these systems, they are ignored, which can result in a proliferation of introns. Keller & Banzhaf (Keller and Banzhaf, 1996) use a repair mechanism of a different sort, whereby illegal terminal symbols in the generated code are replaced with a legal terminal according to a grammar. Each terminal symbol is represented by a unique binary code; an illegal symbol is replaced by the legal symbol whose code is closest by hamming distance. This system also uses fixed-length genomes, in this case with binary coding.

3. GRAMMATICAL EVOLUTION

GE presents a unique way of using grammars in the process of automatic programming. Variable-length binary string genomes are used, with each codon representing an integer value where codons are consecutive groups of 8 bits in order to make the genetic code degenerate. The integer values are used in a mapping function to select an appropriate production rule from the BNF definition; the numbers generated always representing one of the rules that can be used at that time. GE does not suffer from the problem of having to ignore codon integer values because it does not generate illegal values. The issue of ensuring a complete mapping of an individual onto a program comprised exclusively of terminals is partly resolved using a novel technique to evolutionary algorithms called *wrapping*. This technique draws inspiration from the *overlapping genes* phenomenon exhibited by many bacteria, viruses, and mitochondria that enables them to re-use the same genetic material in the expression of different genes (Lewin, 1999).

GE then, is a system that employs a robust new mapping process, the end result of which is the ability to produce code in any language from a simple binary string. At present, the search element of the system is carried out by an evolutionary algorithm, although conceivably any search method with the ability to operate over variable-length binary strings could be employed. In particular, future advances in the field of evolutionary algorithms can be easily incorporated into this system due to the program representation.

3.1 THE BIOLOGICAL APPROACH

The GE system is inspired largely by the biological process of generating a protein from the genetic material of an organism. Proteins are fundamental in the proper development and operation of living organisms and are responsible for traits such as eye colour and height (Lewin, 1999).

Recall from the previous chapter that the genetic material (usually DNA) contains the information required to produce specific proteins at different points along the molecule. For simplicity, consider DNA to be a string of building blocks called nucleotides, of which there are four, named A, T, G, and C, for adenine, tyrosine, guanine, and cytosine respectively. Groups of three nucleotides, called codons, are used to specify the building blocks of proteins. These protein building blocks are known as amino acids, and the sequence of these amino acids in a protein is determined by the sequence of codons on the DNA strand. The sequence of amino acids is very important as it plays a large part in determining the final three-dimensional structure of the protein, which in turn has a role to play in determining its functional properties.

In order to generate a protein from the sequence of nucleotides in the DNA, the nucleotide sequence is first transcribed into a slightly different format, that being a sequence of elements on a molecule known as RNA. Codons within the RNA molecule are then translated to determine the sequence of amino acids that are contained within the protein molecule. The application of production rules to the non-terminals of the incomplete code being mapped in GE is analogous to the role amino acids play when being combined together to transform the growing protein molecule into its final functional three-dimensional form.

The result of the expression of the genetic material as proteins in conjunction with environmental factors is the phenotype. In GE, the phenotype is a computer program that is generated from the genetic material (the genotype) by a process termed a genotype-phenotype mapping. This is unlike the standard method of generating a solution (a program in the case of GE) directly from an individual in an evolutionary algorithm by explicitly encoding the solution within the genetic material. Instead, a many-to-one mapping process is employed within which the robustness of the GE system lies.

Figure 4.1 compares the mapping process employed in both GE and biological organisms.

3.2 THE MAPPING PROCESS

When tackling a problem with GE, a suitable BNF definition must first be decided upon. The BNF can be either the specification of an entire language

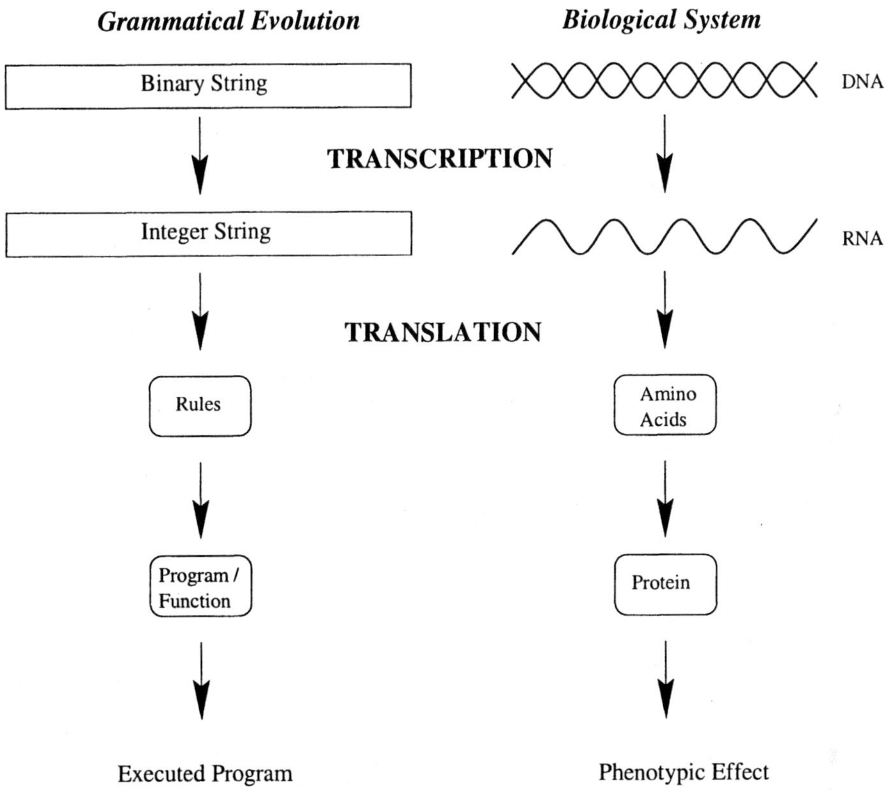

Figure 4.1. A comparison between the grammatical evolution system and a biological genetic system. The binary string of GE is analogous to the double helix of DNA, each guiding the formation of the phenotype. In the case of GE, this occurs via the application of production rules to generate the terminals of the compilable program. In the biological case by directing the formation of the phenotypic protein by determining the order and type of protein subcomponents (amino acids) that are joined together.

or, perhaps more usefully, a subset of a language geared towards the problem at hand. Complete BNFs are freely available for languages such as C, and these can be plugged into GE.

3.2.1 BACKUS NAUR FORM

In GE, a BNF definition (see Section 4.2.1) is used to describe the output language to be produced by the system. This language can subsequently be used for compilation, or interpreted, and consists of elements from the terminal set T. The grammar is used in a developmental approach whereby the evolutionary process evolves the production rules to be applied at each stage of a mapping process, starting from the start symbol, until a complete program is formed. A complete program is one that is comprised solely from elements of T.

As the BNF definition is a plug-in component of the system, it means that GE can produce code in any language thereby giving the system a unique flexibility.

Below is an example BNF definition, where

$$N = \{expr, op, pre\_op, var\}$$

$$T = \{Sin, +, -, /, *, X, 1.0, (,)\}$$

$$S = expr$$

And P can be represented as:

```
(A) <expr> ::= <expr> <op> <expr>       (0)
             | ( <expr> <op> <expr> )   (1)
             | <pre-op> ( <expr> )      (2)
             | <var>                    (3)

(B) <op> ::= +        (0)
           | -        (1)
           | /        (2)
           | *        (3)
(C) <pre-op> ::= Sin
(D) <var> ::= X       (0)
            | 1.0     (1)
```

As noted earlier in Section 4.2.1, there is the possibility of confusion with the terminology adopted with grammars and the GP terms **GPFunctions** and **GPTerminals**. In GE, we use the term **terminals** with its usual meaning in the context of grammars.

For the above BNF, Table 4.1 summarizes the production rules and the number of choices associated with each.

Table 4.1. The number of choices available from each production rule.

Rule no.	*Choices*
A	4
B	4
C	1
D	2

3.2.2 MAPPING PROCESS OUTLINE

The genotype is used to map the start symbol onto terminals by reading codons of 8 bits to generate a corresponding integer value, from which an appropriate production rule is selected by using the following mapping function:

$$Rule = (Codon\ integer\ value)$$
$$MOD$$
$$(Number\ of\ rules\ for\ the\ current\ non-terminal)$$

Consider the following rule i.e., given the non-terminal *op* there are four production rules to select from.

```
(B) <op> :: = +          (0)
            | -          (1)
            | /          (2)
            | *          (3)
```

If we assume the codon being read produces the integer 6, then

$$6\ MOD\ 4\ =\ 2$$

would select rule (2) **<op> ::= /**. Each time a production rule has to be selected to transform a non-terminal, another codon is read. In this way the system traverses the genome.

During the genotype-to-phenotype mapping process it is possible for individuals to run out of codons, and in this case we wrap the individual and reuse the codons. This is quite an unusual approach in EAs, as it is entirely possible for certain codons to be used two or more times. This technique of wrapping the individual draws inspiration from the gene-overlapping phenomenon that has been observed in many organisms (Lewin, 1999).

In GE, each time the same codon is expressed it will always generate the same integer value, but, depending on the current non-terminal to which it is being applied, it may result in the selection of a different production rule. What is crucial, however, is that each time a particular individual is mapped from its genotype to its phenotype, the same output is generated. This is the case because the same choices are made each time. However, it is possible that an incomplete mapping could occur, even after several wrapping events, and in this case the individual in question is given the lowest possible fitness value. The selection and replacement mechanisms then operate accordingly to increase the likelihood that this individual is removed from the population.

An incomplete mapping could arise if the integer values expressed by the genotype were applying the same production rules repeatedly. For example, consider an individual with three codons, all of which specify rule 0 from below,

```
(A) <expr> :: = <expr><op><expr>          (0)
              | (<expr><op><expr>)        (1)
              | <pre-op>(<expr>)          (2)
              | <var>                     (3)
```

even after wrapping the mapping process would be incomplete and would carry on indefinitely unless stopped. This occurs because the non-terminal `<expr>` is being mapped recursively by production rule 0, i.e., it becomes `<expr><op><expr>`. Therefore, the leftmost `<expr>` after each application of a production would itself be mapped to a `<expr><op><expr>`, resulting in an expression continually growing as follows:
`<expr><op><expr><op><expr><op><expr>` etc.

Such an individual is dubbed invalid as it will never undergo a complete mapping to a set of terminals. It is clearly essential that stop sequences are found during the evolutionary search in order to complete the mapping process to a functional program. The stop sequence being a set of codons that result in the non-terminals being transformed into elements of the grammars terminal set.

Beginning from the left hand side of the genome then, codon integer values are generated and used to select rules from the BNF grammar, until one of the following situations arise:

1 A complete program is generated. This occurs when all the non-terminals in the expression being mapped are transformed into elements from the terminal set of the BNF grammar.

2 The end of the genome is reached, in which case the *wrapping* operator is invoked. This results in the return of the genome reading frame to the left hand side of the genome once again. The reading of codons will then continue, unless an upper threshold representing the maximum number of wrapping events has occurred during this individual's mapping process.

3 In the event that a threshold on the number of wrapping events has occurred and the individual is still incompletely mapped, the mapping process is halted, and the individual is assigned the lowest possible fitness value.

3.3 EXAMPLE INDIVIDUAL

Consider the individual in Figure 4.2. These numbers will be used to look up the Table 4.1 that describes the BNF grammar given in Section 3.2.1.

Concentrating on the start symbol `<expr>`, we can see that there are four productions to choose from.

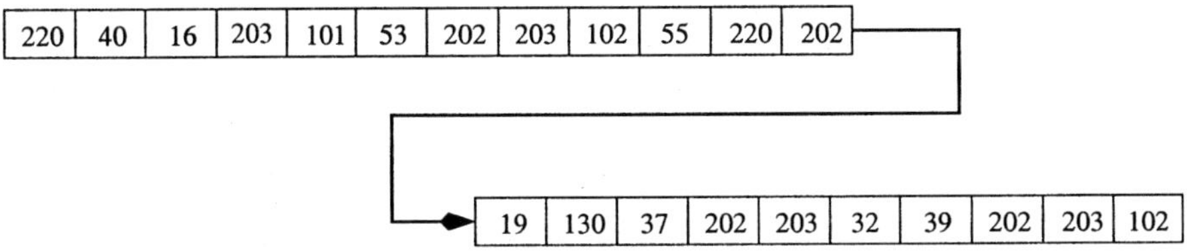

Figure 4.2. An example individual expressed as integers. The integer values are generated by converting the 8-bit binary number that is each codon into its corresponding integer value.

```
(A) <expr> : : = <expr><op><expr>          (0)
               | (<expr><op><expr>)        (1)
               | <pre-op>(<expr>)          (2)
               | <var>                     (3)
```

To make this choice, we read the first codon from the chromosome and use it to generate a number. This number will then be used to decide which production rule to use, according to the mapping function given in Section 3.2.2. We have 220 $MOD\ 4 = 0$, meaning we must take the first production (A.0)[1], so that `<expr>` is now replaced with

```
<expr><op><expr>
```

Notice that if this individual is subsequently wrapped each codon will always result in the same integer value, but, depending on the number of choices for the current non-terminal, a different rule number could be selected. In this way, although we have the same codon integer value, it could result in a different physical trait.

Continuing with the first `<expr>`, i.e., always starting from the left-most non-terminal, a similar choice must be made by reading the next codon value (40), and again using the given formula we get 40 $MOD\ 4 = 0$, that is rule (A.0). The left-most `<expr>` will now be replaced with `<expr><op><expr>` to give

```
<expr><op><expr><op><expr>
```

For a third time, we have the same choice for the first `<expr>`, by reading the next codon value 16, the result being the application of rule (A.0) to give

```
<expr><op><expr><op><expr><op><expr>
```

Now the left-most `<expr>` will be determined by the codon value 203 which gives us rule (A.3) which is `<expr>` becomes `<var>`, resulting in

[1] Production rules are represented here as X.Y, where X represents the non-terminal, and Y represents the rule to be applied to the non-terminal X.

```
<var><op><expr><op><expr><op><expr>
```

The next codon then determines what value <var>, which has two possible production rules, shall take, i.e.,

```
(D) <var> ::= X         (0)
            | 1.0       (1)
```

This gives us 101 $MOD\ 2 = 1$ i.e., rule (D.1), which turns out to be **1.0**. We now have the following

```
1.0 <op><expr><op><expr><op><expr>
```

The next codon will determine what <op> will become, so we have 53 $MOD\ 4 = 1$, which is **<op> ::= -**. The next <expr> has then to be expanded using the codon value 202, that is 202 $MOD\ 4 = 2$. So we now have

```
1.0-<pre-op>(<expr>)<op><expr><op><expr>
```

There can only be one outcome for a <pre-op> that being **Sin**, therefore, no decision has to be made and so no codon is read. The next <expr> is then expanded by the value 203 $MOD\ 4 = 3$ which is rule (A.3), or <var> . The value <var> takes is then determined by 102 $MOD\ 2 = 0$, rule (D.0), and the resulting expression is

```
1.0 - Sin(x)<op><expr><op><expr>
```

The mapping continues until eventually, we are left with the following expression:

```
1.0 - Sin(x)*Sin(x) - Sin(x)*Sin(x)
```

Notice how all of the codons were required in this case, had there been any extra codons they would have been simply ignored. If we had run out of codons we would have wrapped back to the first codon and continued reading codons until one of the termination conditions, outlined in Section 3.2.2, were met.

3.4 GENETIC CODE DEGENERACY

Given an 8-bit binary number, each codon in GE can represent 256 distinct integer values, although many of these integer values can represent the same production rule. Taking production rule 2 in Section 3.2.1 as an example, if the current codon value were 8, then 8 $MOD\ 4 = 0$ would select rule $(B.0)$, that is, **<op> ::= +**.

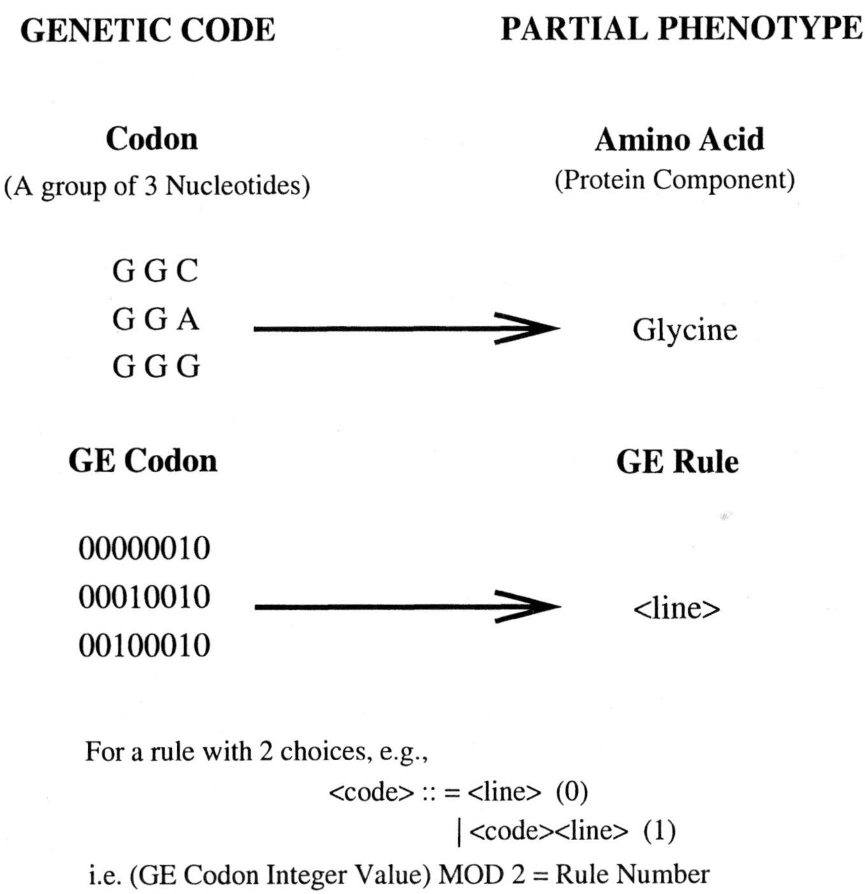

Figure 4.3. Genetic code degeneracy in GE (bottom) compared to the biological genetic code (top). In the case of the biological genetic code, we can see 3 sets of codons representing the same protein component, Glycine. These codons differ only in the base at the third position. In the example GE codons, again we see different codons representing the same production rule from the grammar definition.

The same rule would be chosen if the codon value were 4, 12, 16, etc.

A similar phenomenon can be observed in the genetic code of biological organisms, referred to as *degenerate genetic code* (Lewin, 1999). Some discussion on this topic is conducted in chapter 3. There are 4^3, i.e., 64, unique combinations of nucleotides in a codon, 61 of these coding for a specific amino acid, the other three are special codons that delimit the start and end of genes on the DNA. On average, there are three codons for every amino acid, that is, more than one codon can represent the same amino acid. It has been observed that the first two nucleotides in the codon are often sufficient to specify a particular amino acid, the value of the nucleotide at the third position often being irrelevant. Code degeneracy has interesting implications when it comes to mutation effects. A mutation at the third codon position can often produce what is called a *neutral mutation*, meaning that the amino acid specified will be the same as the one before the mutation event due to the flexibility at the third codon position. With respect to GE, this means that subtle changes in the search space (genotype) may have no effect on the solution space (phenotype), which could result in the maintenance of genotypic diversity throughout a run of the system as different genotypes can represent the same phenotype. It may also preserve valid individuals because the neutral mutations provide a buffering effect against destructive mutation events. Evidence to this effect has been presented in (O'Neill and Ryan, 1999b). Later, advantages of neutrality in the evolution of digital circuits and another GP variant has been discussed (Vassilev and Miller, 2000; Miller and Thomson, 2000). Figure 4.3 shows that in the genetic code of biological organisms, the nucleotide at the third position of the codon is independent of the amino acid produced (Glycine). Similarly with GE, it can be seen in the given example that a single bit mutation has no effect on the rule used in this case. For a grammar rule with two choices,

```
<code>:: = <line>         (0)
         | <code><line> (1)
```

e.g., $2\ MOD\ 2 = 18\ MOD\ 2 = 34\ MOD\ 2 = 0$, all specify rule 0. Note, however, if the number of choices in the example was uneven, e.g., three, a single bit mutation would effect the rule used.

Kimura's neutral theory of evolution (Kimura, 1983) suggests that it is these neutral mutations which are responsible for the genetic diversity that has been observed in natural populations, a feature that has been exhibited within GE.

3.5 THE SEARCH ALGORITHM

We adopt an evolutionary algorithm to perform a search of the program solution space by indirectly operating on variable-length, binary strings. Conceivably any search algorithm that can operate on binary or integer strings could employ GE's mapping process to generate a program. As the population being evolved comprises simple binary strings, we do not have to employ any special crossover or mutation operators, and an unconstrained search is performed on these strings due to the genotype-to-phenotype mapping process that will generate syntactically correct individuals.

The evolutionary algorithm adopted in this case is a variable-length genetic algorithm. Individual initialisation is achieved by randomly generating variable-length binary strings within a pre-specified range of codons. For all experiments conducted in this paper we use the initialisation range of one to ten codons, where a codon is a group of eight bits.

As well as the standard genetic operators of mutation (point) and crossover (one-point) we adopt a codon duplication operator. Duplication involves randomly selecting a number of codons to duplicate and the starting position of the first codon in this set. The duplicated codons are placed at the penultimate codon position at the end of the chromosome so as to facilitate their incorporation into the phenotype. We do this because if the the individual produced a completely mapped program after reading the last codon, and we placed duplicated codons after this point, they will not be used by this individual, until some other genetic operator allowed them to be switched on.

The GE component of the system, that is, the part that carries out the mapping from binary string to the output code, could conceivably be plugged-in to the fitness function of any EA. The result of this is that GE can benefit from the latest advances in EA research, for example, future investigations will be conducted into the use of competent GAs that have been shown to have superior scaling properties to the simple GA (Goldberg, 2002; Goldberg et al., 1989; Thierens, 1999; Harik and Goldberg, 1997; Harik, 1999; Kargupta, 1998; Pelikan et al., 2000).

4. DISCUSSION

In chapter 3 we described a number of desirable features that an evolutionary automatic programming system could avail of based on our lessons from Molecular Biology. Given the description above of GE, it can be seen that we have taken advantage of a number of these features, i.e., the first six of eight. Specifically,

1 We achieved a generalised encoding that can represent a variety of structures. We do this by using a separation of the search and solution spaces through the use of a genotype-phenotype distinction. The transformation or mapping process allows us to use a BNF grammar definition as a plug-in component of the system, the BNF being a generalised encoding of the structures we are evolving, i.e., programs. This allows us to generate programs in an arbitrary language. The genotype-phenotype distinction in turn facilitates the following five features.

2 The potential of efficiency gains for the evolutionary search have been achieved with the use of a degenerate genetic code. The existence of the degenerate genetic code means that neutral mutation events are possible, and therefore neutral evolution can occur. As discussed in chapter 3, this is reported to have benefits for the efficiency of the evolutionary search.

3 Following on from the existence of the degenerate genetic code, the potential for the maintenance of genetic diversity exists. In the above system description 8-bit codons are used to represent integers values. A property of the mapping function is that it is redundant, giving rise to what we call the degeneracy property, thus different integer values can represent the same grammar production rule. Consequently, different genotypes can represent the same phenotype, thus facilitating genetic diversity within a population.

4 Preservation of functionality is also aided by virtue of the degenerate genetic code. As discussed in chapter 3, neutral mutation events can occur that change the genotype but may not result in a phenotypic change.

5 With the introduction of the wrapping operator we have provided a facility whereby re-use of genetic material is possible. In the event that an individual is incompletely mapped upon reaching the last codon on a genome, the wrapping operator allows the re-use of codons at the beginning of the genome.

6 A compression of representation can be facilitated as a direct result of the wrapping operator. An investigation into this fact will be conducted in chapter 6.

Investigations as part of an analysis of GE, conducted in chapter 6, will demonstrate the existence of features 2, 3, 4, 5 and 6.

The seventh feature of gene expression regulation through transcription is implemented in a very simple fashion, whereby, groups of eight bits are read starting from the first bit on the chromosome until the end of the chromosome is reached, unless wrapping occurs. A future avenue for investigation would be to modify the transcription process to allow alternative reading frames, and an operon-like expression regulation framework.

The eighth feature of positional independence is not fully realised in the current setup of GE, in that a codon integer value will have as many meanings as contexts in which it can be used. That is, if there are four non-terminals in the grammar, then each codon could have a meaning for each non-terminal. By employing alternative translation strategies to the simple mod of the number of rules for a non-terminal it would be possible to investigate position independence. Chapter 8 considers this avenue of investigation.

5. CONCLUSIONS

We have presented the Grammatical Evolution (GE) system and described its operation and unique features. In the next chapter we present proof of concept problems that demonstrate GE's ability to generate code in an arbitrary language and also conduct a comparison with GP.

Chapters 6 and 7 will then report on an analysis of GE, including the degenerate genetic code, the wrapping operator, and the role that crossover plays in the system.

Chapter 5

FOUR EXAMPLES OF GRAMMATICAL EVOLUTION

1. INTRODUCTION

We now describe the application of GE to a number of problem domains, namely a symbolic regression problem, a symbolic integration problem, the Santa Fe ant trail, and the evolution of caching algorithms. These problems are deliberately diverse; for example, in the symbolic regression problem a simple one-line expression is evolved, whereas in the Santa Fe trail problem a multiline function including branch statements is required.

As outlined in the previous chapter, all that is required to apply GE to each of these problems is a grammar and a fitness function, to specify syntactically legal individuals and to test their semantic suitability respectively.

A description of each problem domain used now follows, including a report on the performance of GE, and a comparison with results obtained by GP for these problem domains is also provided.

2. SYMBOLIC REGRESSION

Symbolic regression problems involve finding some mathematical expression in symbolic form that represents a given set of input and output pairs. The aim is to determine the function that maps the input pairs onto the output pairs. The particular function examined is

$$f(X) = X^4 + X^3 + X^2 + X$$

with the input values in the range $[-1, +1]$.

The grammar used in this problem is given below:

$$N = \{expr, op, pre\_op, var\}$$

$$T = \{sin, cos, exp, log, +, -, /, *, X, 1.0, (,)\}$$

$$S = expr$$

And P can be represented as:

```
(1) <expr> ::= <expr> <op> <expr>         (0)
             | ( <expr> <op> <expr> )     (1)
             | <pre-op> ( <expr> )        (2)
             | <var>                      (3)

(2) <op> ::= +          (0)
           | -          (1)
           | /          (2)
           | *          (3)

(3) <pre-op> ::= sin     (0)
               | cos     (1)
               | exp     (2)
               | log     (3)

(4) <var> ::= X         (0)
            | 1.0       (1)
```

The production rules for <expr> are similar to those given earlier in Section 3.2.1, with the terminal operator set also including Cos, Exp, and Log.

The fitness for this problem is given by the sum, taken over 20 fitness cases, of the error between the evolved and target functions. Tableaus for GP and GE can be seen in Tables 5.1 and 5.2, respectively.

Table 5.1. A Koza-style tableau for Symbolic Regression

Objective:	Find a function of one independent variable and one dependent variable, in symbolic form that fits a given sample of 20 (x_i, y_i) data points, where the target functions is the quartic polynomial $X^4 + X^3 + X^2 + X$
GPTerminal Set:	X (the independent variable)
GPFunction Set:	$+, -, *, \%$, sin, cos, exp, log
Fitness cases:	The given sample of 20 data points in the interval $[-1, +1]$
Raw Fitness:	The sum, taken over the 20 fitness cases, of the error
Standardised Fitness:	Same as raw fitness
Hits:	The number of fitness cases for which the error is less than 0.01
Wrapper:	None
Parameters:	$M = 500$, $G = 51$

Table 5.2. Symbolic Regression Tableau for GE

Objective:	Find a function of one independent variable and one dependent variable, in symbolic form that fits a given sample of 20 (x_i, y_i) data points, where the target function is the quartic polynomial $X^4 + X^3 + X^2 + X$
Terminal Operands:	X (the independent variable), 1.0
Terminal Operators:	The binary operators $+, *, /,$ and $-$ The unary operators sin, cos, exp and log
Fitness cases:	The given sample of 20 data points in the interval $[-1, +1]$
Raw Fitness:	The sum, taken over the 20 fitness cases, of the error
Standardised Fitness:	Same as raw fitness
Wrapper:	Standard productions to generate C functions
Parameters:	Population Size = 500, Termination when Generations = 51 Prob. Mutation = 0.01, Prob. Crossover = 0.9 Prob. Duplication = 0.01, Steady State

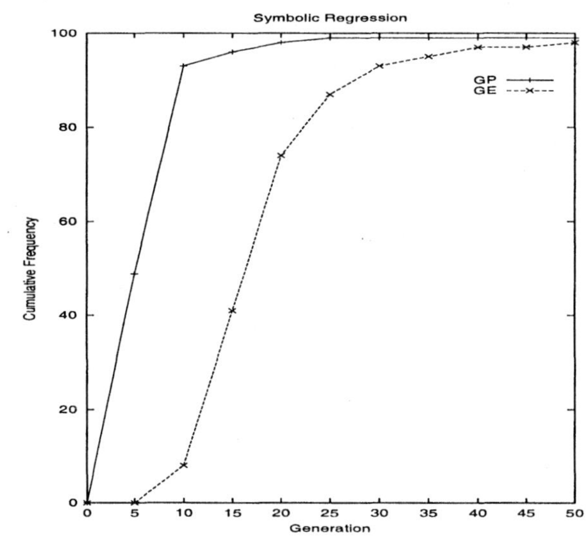

Figure 5.1. Cumulative frequency of success measure of GE versus GP on the symbolic regression problem.

2.1 RESULTS

GE successfully found the $X + X^2 + X^3 + X^4$ target function. A cumulative frequency measure of success over 100 runs can be seen in Figure 5.1, along with a similar measure for GP, and in this case GP outperforms GE, particularly early on in the run. In fact, it is only after five generations that GE discovers any correct solutions, while GP is, at that stage, achieving a cumulative frequency of success of over 90%. Section 3.1 suggests some reasons why there is such a disparity for this particular problem.

3. SYMBOLIC INTEGRATION

Symbolic integration involves finding a function that is the integral of the given curve. Similarly to symbolic regression the system is given a set of input and output pairs and must determine the function that maps one onto the other. The particular function examined was

$$f(X) = cos(X) + 2X + 1$$

with the input values in the range $[0, 2\pi]$ and the target integral curve being

$$f(X) = sin(X) + X + X^2$$

In a manner similar to Koza (Koza, 1992), we reduce the problem to symbolic regression by integrating the function examined and performing symbolic regression on the target integral curve. The fitness for this problem is given by the sum, taken over 20 fitness cases, of the absolute value of the difference between the individual genetically produced function $f_j(x_i)$ at the domain point x_i and the value of the numerical integral $\mathbf{I}(x_i)$.

The grammar used for this problem is the same as for the symbolic regression problem given in section 2, and a tableau for GE is given in Table 5.3. For comparison the corresponding GP tableau is included in Table 5.4.

3.1 RESULTS

GE successfully found the target integral function $sin(X) + X + X^2$ illustrating that useful expressions could be generated by the system. A cumulative frequency measure of success over 100 runs can be seen in Figure 5.2. The same problem was tackled using GP and a cumulative frequency of success for 100 runs can be seen in Figure 5.2. As can be seen GE outperforms GP on this problem from around the 10th generation.

When comparing GE to GP, it is important to note how the initial generation is formed in each system. In the case of the GP system a ramped half-and-half generation mechanism is used, creating a range of individuals of varying shapes and depths, whereas with GE the generation is totally random. Also, every individual in the initial population is engineered to be unique in the GP system, whereas with GE this is not the case. In the case of this problem we feel that the generation strategy for the initial generation is providing GP with an advantage due to the regular nature of the solution, as illustrated in Figure 5.3, and by the number of successful solutions in early generations, see Figure 5.1.

Table 5.3. Symbolic Integration Tableau for GE

Objective:	Find a function, in symbolic form, that is the integral of a curve presented either as a mathematical expression or as a given finite sample of points (x_i, y_i)
Terminal Operands:	X (the independent variable)
Terminal Operators:	The binary operators $+, *, /, -$ and the unary operators sin, cos, exp and log
Fitness cases:	A sample of 20 data points in the interval $[0, 2\pi]$
Raw Fitness	The sum, taken over the 20 fitness cases, of the absolute value of the difference between the individual genetically produced function $f_j(x_i)$ at the domain point x_i and the value of the numerical integral $\mathbf{I}(x_i)$
Standardised Fitness:	Same as raw fitness
Wrapper:	Standard productions to generate C functions
Parameters:	Population Size = 500, Termination when Generations = 51 Prob. Mutation = 0.01, Prob. Crossover = 0.9 Prob. Duplication = 0.01, Steady State

Table 5.4. A Koza-style tableau for Symbolic Integration

Objective:	Find a function, in symbolic form, that is the integral of a curve presented either as a mathematical expression or as a given finite sample of points (x_i, y_i)
GPTerminal Set:	X (the independent variable)
GPFunction Set:	$+, -, *, \%, \sin, \cos, \exp, \log$
Fitness cases:	The given sample of 50 data points in the interval $[0, 2\pi]$
Raw Fitness:	The sum, taken over the 50 fitness cases, of the absolute value of the difference between the individual genetically produced function $f_j(x_i)$ at the domain point x_i and the value of the numerical integral $\mathbf{I}(x_i)$
Standardised Fitness:	Same as raw fitness
Hits:	The number of fitness cases for which the error is less than 0.01
Wrapper:	None
Parameters:	$M = 500, G = 51$

Additional support is provided by the fact that on the symbolic integration problem the solution does not have the same regularity as is the case here, see Figure 5.4.

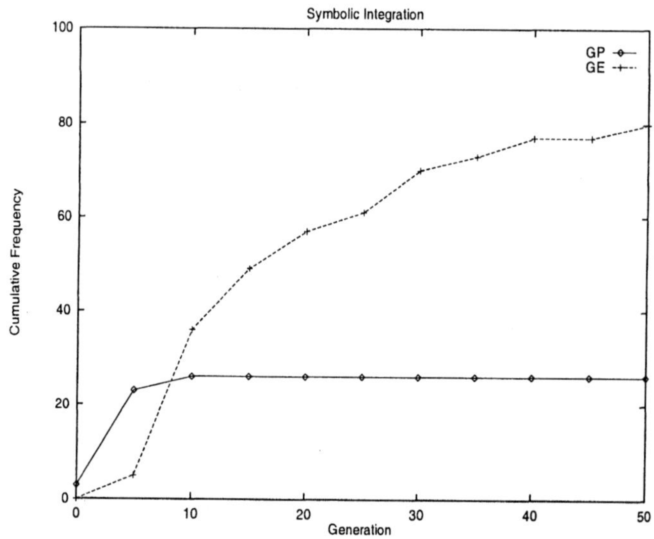

Figure 5.2. Cumulative frequency of success measure of GE versus GP on the symbolic integration problem.

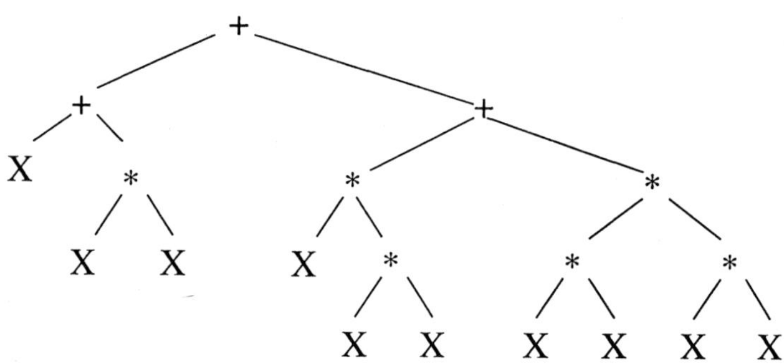

Figure 5.3. Example solution to Symbolic Regression as a GP parse tree. Note the regular, repetitive nature of the solution.

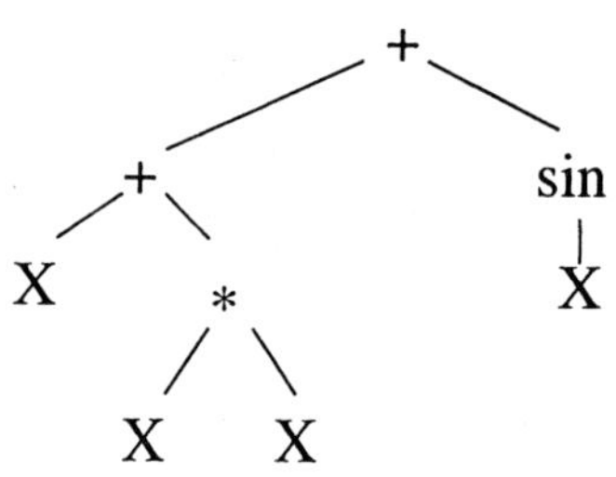

Figure 5.4. Example solution to Symbolic Integration as a GP parse tree.

The random nature of GE initialisation and the apparent utility of the ramped half-and-half approach is discussed in chapter 8 where a new form of initialisation for GE is described, *Sensible Initialisation*.

4. SANTA FE ANT TRAIL

The Santa Fe ant trail is a standard problem in the area of GP and can be considered a deceptive planning problem with many local and global optima (Langdon and Poli, 1998). The objective is to find a computer program to control an artificial ant so that it can find all 89 pieces of food located on a non-continuous trail within a specified number of time steps, the trail being located on a 32 by 32 toroidal grid. The ant can turn left, right, move one square forward, and may also look ahead one square in the direction it is facing to determine if that square contains a piece of food. All actions, with the exception of looking ahead for food, take one time step to execute. The ant starts in the top left-hand corner of the grid facing the first piece of food on the trail. The grammar used in this problem is different to the ones used for symbolic integration and symbolic regression. In this problem we wish to produce a multiline function, as opposed to a single line expression. The grammar used is given below:

$$N = \{code, line, expr, if - statement, op\}$$

$$T = \{left(), right(), move(), food\_ahead(),$$
$$else, if, \{, \}, (,), ;\}$$

$$S = code$$

And P can be represented as:

```
(1) <code> :: =  <line>                (0)
                |<code><line>          (1)

(2) <line> :: =  <if-statement>        (0)
                |<op>                  (1)

(3) <if-statement> :: = if(food_ahead())
                          {<line>}
                        else
                          {<line>}

(4) <op> :: =      left();              (0)
                 | right();             (1)
                 | move();              (2)
```

Table 5.5. Grammatical Evolution Tableau for the Santa Fe Trail

Objective:	Find a computer program to control an artificial ant so that it can find all 89 pieces of food located on the Santa Fe Trail.
Terminal Operators:	left(), right(), move(), food_ahead()
Terminal Operands:	None
Fitness cases:	One fitness case
Raw Fitness:	Number of pieces of food before the ant times out with 615 operations.
Standardised Fitness:	Total number of pieces of food less the raw fitness.
Wrapper:	None
Parameters:	Population Size = 500, Termination when Generations = 51 Prob. Mutation = 0.01, Prob. Crossover = 0.9 Prob. Duplication = 0.01, Steady State

Note that it is the rules for the non-terminal `<code>` that are responsible for the production of multiline code. A tableau describing this problem can be seen in Table 5.5.

4.1 RESULTS

GE was successful at finding a solution to this case of the Santa Fe trail, demonstrating that GE can generate multiline code by using a simple modification to the grammar definition. An example solution produced by GE is:

```
move();
left();
if(food_ahead())
    left();
else
    right();
right();
if(food_ahead())
    move();
else
    left();
```

which is executed in a loop until the number of time steps allowed is reached. A cumulative frequency measure of success over 100 runs of GE can be seen in Figure 5.5. This figure also shows the performance of the GP system, which incorporated solution length in the fitness measure, as well as the number of pieces of food picked up, as follows:

$$Fitness = Food\ Picked\ Up + \frac{(Solution\ Length)^2}{1000}$$

The fitness of a GE individual, on the other hand, was simply the number of food pieces picked up. The performance of the two systems is comparable in this case with GP slightly outperforming GE over the first 30 generations.

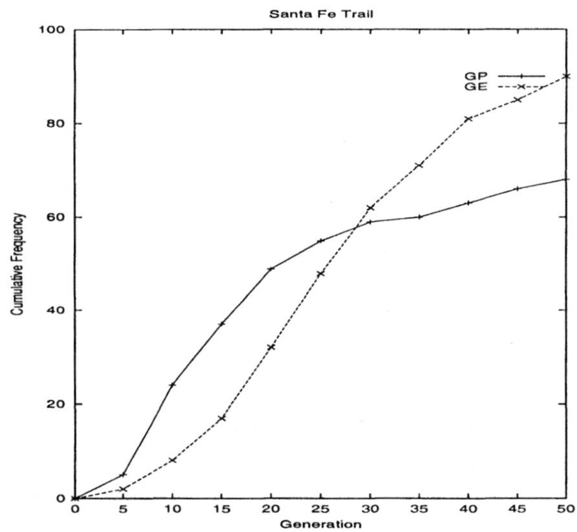

Figure 5.5. The cumulative frequency of success measure for GE versus GP on the Santa Fe trail problem. The results show the case when GP uses solution length in the fitness function (GE has no such measure).

In order to see how the GP system would perform without the solution length as a measure of fitness, we ran 100 more runs of the GP system removing the solution length measure. We felt that using solution length as a measure of fitness required a prior knowledge of the solution's length and therefore gave an unfair advantage, as GE did not use such a measure. Figure 5.6 shows a comparison of the cumulative frequency measure of success for these results with the results produced by GE. As can be seen from the figure the performance of the GP system was compromised and as a result GE outperformed GP.

5. CACHING ALGORITHMS

We now describe how GE was applied to the real world problem of evolving a Caching Algorithm, at which GP has been found to generate algorithms that did not perform as well as those designed by humans (Paterson and Livesey, 1997; O'Neill and Ryan, 1999a).

A cache memory is a small, fast memory, ideally into which the *address space* of a running program is held in order to improve efficiency of the program's

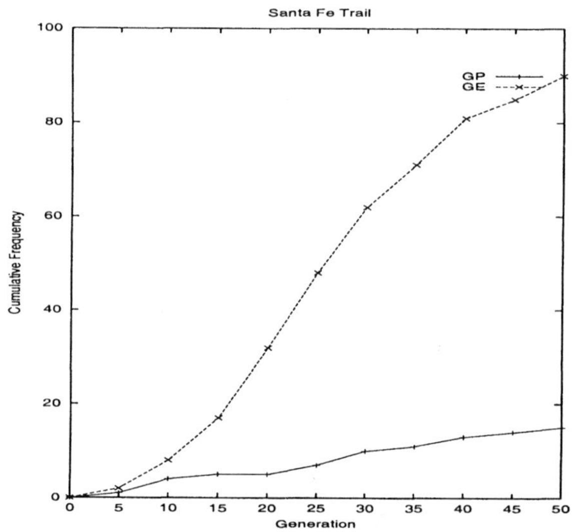

Figure 5.6. The cumulative frequency of success measure for GE versus GP on the Santa Fe trail problem. The results shown illustrate the case where the solution length constraint is removed from GP.

execution. Caches operate on the notion of *locality of reference*; that is, if a word in memory has recently been accessed, it is likely to be required again soon. The executing program generates a stream of *requests* of main memory locations to access. A recording of this request stream is referred to as a *trace*. The cache has a fixed number of *lines* each of which can hold a word (an address). When a *request* is met from the cache memory this is called a *hit*, otherwise a *miss* occurs. In the event of a miss, the requested memory location is copied into the cache to the first empty *line* available, otherwise a caching algorithm determines which line of the cache will be replaced (the *victim*). In order that the caching algorithm can make an educated decision as to which line will become the victim, typically some management information is available, e.g. an ordered list of lines.

For the purposes of these experiments, we adhered as closely as possible to the procedures outlined in (Paterson and Livesey, 1997), in order to facilitate a comparison of the systems. Thus, the same trace files, a similar grammar (no default or multiple rules were used) with the same terminal set, an integer management array `info[]` (one element per line), and the same fitness function were used. The raw fitness of a caching algorithm is therefore given as

$$number\ of\ runs - number\ of\ misses$$

where a run is a consecutive series of identical requests.

Table 5.6. Available terminal operators.

Terminal Operator	*Function*
$write\_x(i, v)$:	sets info[i] to v
$read\_x(i)$:	returns info[i]
$small\_x(i, v)$:	index of smallest element of info[]
$large\_x(i, v)$:	index of largest element of info[]
$random\_x(i, v)$:	index of random element of info[]
$counter()$:	successive values 0, 1, 2 etc
$div(x, y)$:	if y==0 then 1 else x / y
$rem(x, y)$:	if y==0 then 1 else x % y

The terminal operators and their respective functions are given in Table 5.6.The grammar as adopted in most of the experiments described in the next section is as follows:

```
(1)  <stmts> :: = <stmt>
                | <stmt>;<stmts>

(2)  <stmt> :: = if(<expr>){<stmts>;}else{<stmts>;}
               | write_x(<expr>,<expr>);
               | victim=<expr>;

(3)  <expr> :: = <term>
               | <term>+<term>
               | <term>-<term>
               | <term>*<term>
               | div(<term>,<term>)
               | rem(<term>,<term>)

(4)  <term> :: = CACHESIZE
               | <num>
               | <fun>
               | (<expr>)

(5)  <num> :: = <mant>
              | <mant><zeros>

(6)  <mant> :: = 0 | 1 | 2 | 5

(7)  <zeros> :: = 0 | 0<zeros>
```

```
(8)  <fun>  ::= counter()
              | read_x(<expr>)
              | small_x()
              | large_x()
              | random_x()
```

5.1 RESULTS

Similar to Paterson and Livesley (Paterson and Livesey, 1997), we employ three trace files from Flanagan (Flanagan et al., 1992). One file is used for training GE, while the resulting algorithms are tested using the other two. The training file `ken2.00200` contains around 400,000 requests with about 250,000 distinct addresses. Paterson and Livesley reduced memory requirements by eliminating the lower order 10 bits of each addresses, thus reducing the alphabet size to just 500, i.e. 500 distinct addresses as opposed to 250,000 originally. We use the files in their original state, and show comparisons with Paterson and Livesley's algorithm below. Paterson and Livesley found that the speed of the cache simulator frustrated his attempts to run many experiments, and we suffered the same experience. To alleviate this, we use a population of just 50 individuals, compared to his 500. For each of the experiments that follow, ten runs were conducted, and the best individual at the end of twenty generations was analysed.

Small Cachesize.

The first experiment consists of using a cache size of just 20, which, given that the training file contains 250,000 distinct addresses, makes it very difficult to exploit any locality of reference. The best individual generated by GE was

```
GE 1 :        victim = counter() - CACHESIZE;
```

This curious looking individual simply cycles through the cache when searching for a victim, selecting it without consideration for how recently it was used. There is, however, an implicit temporal quality about the manner in which victims are selected. A word is guaranteed to remain in the cache for at least `CACHESIZE` requests, longer if it (or other cache members) is requested. This outperforms the human designed Least Recently Used algorithm (LRU) by 15.7%, and, by virtue of its simplicity, is far less expensive to use.

Large Cachesize.

A cachesize of 200 lines was used in this instance, and one of the best individuals produced was again GE 1. However, in this case the number of misses was far less, outperforming LRU by 46.2%.

Using info [ ].

Given the level of disinterest exhibited by GE in the use of the `info[]` array, we ran an experiment that forced it to write into some element before choosing its victim. The grammar in this case varied from the one outlined above in the case of the production rules for the non-terminals `stmts` and `stmt`. Both of these rules were replaced with the following:

```
(1)  <stmts> :: = write_x(<expr>,<expr>); victim=<expr>;
```

The best of run individual generated by this system was:

```
GE 2 : write_x( CACHESIZE + counter(),
                CACHESIZE + counter())
       victim = CACHESIZE + counter();
```

Rather predictably, this individual simply ignores what it writes into the array, and promptly chooses its victim using the same method as in the other experiments. In fact, the ubiquity of the beautifully simple `CACHESIZE+counter()` algorithm is demonstrated by virtue of its appearance in no less than three parts of this algorithm.

Constants.

Paterson and Livesley reported on an experiment where the use of constants was prohibited. He was pleased to note that imposing this restriction actually improved the performance of their system. In no case did GE produce an individual that required constants, and it appears that the system discovered that constants were unnecessary in this case, giving a nice example of how Evolutionary methods will always take the path of least resistance.

Comparison of Algorithms.

A comparison between the LRU algorithm and those which had been evolved was carried out by rating their performance on the other two (unseen) trace files, and the number of misses obtained in each case can be seen in Table 5.7.

Paterson and Livesley were dismayed to report that the algorithms they produced were very poor at generalising to unseen data, and that they suffered greatly from overfitting. The algorithms produced by GE don't suffer from this problem, and perform extremely well on the new data. One factor that might contribute to the large difference in performance was Paterson and Livesley's decision to simplify the problem - the problem as posed to GE was possibly too large to spot any patterns in, while the other system suffered from a degree of overfitting.

The solution generated by GE was so general that when applied to a larger cache size, a huge increase in performance was observed. When the cache size was increased by an order of magnitude for LRU, the accompanying increase in

Table 5.7. Algorithm performance comparison.

Algorithm (Cachesize)	*ken2.00100 (Misses)*	*ken2.00200 (Misses)*	*Average of % Improvement over LRU*
LRU (20)	374,596	380,041	-
LRU (200)	367,104	373,935	-
GE1 (20)	300,569	318,444	17.97
GE1 (200)	106,067	82,856	74.51
GE2 (20)	300,569	318,445	17.97
GE2 (200)	106,068	82,855	74.51

performance shows that the associated cost of such an increase would probably not pay off.

Simplified Stream Data.
Another set of experiments were conducted to determine if using the simplified data stream as adopted in (Paterson and Livesey, 1997) would have a detrimental effect on the generalisation capabilities of solutions found by GE. Similarly to Paterson and Livesley we removed the low-order 10 bits from each address in the training stream file, thus reducing the alphabet size to 500 as opposed to 250,000 in the original stream.

Experiments with the small cachesize, large cachesize and forcing the solutions to write to the info[] array were conducted, and in each case GE rediscovered the solutions found in the original experiments. Simplifying the training data set thus had no effect on the generalisation capabilities of GE.

6. CONCLUSIONS

We have presented a number of proof of concept problems that have been successfully tackled by GE. The reported results demonstrate GE's ability to generate compilable code in any language using its unique genotype-phenotype mapping process. In accordance with the No Free Lunch theorem, we do not expect GE to be good at all problems. However, we have demonstrated GE's ability to solve a diverse set of problems, and a comparison of performance to GP, has shown GE to be on a par, and in some cases superior to GP. We now proceed by conducting an analysis of GE on some of the problem domains reported in this chapter.

Chapter 6

ANALYSIS OF GRAMMATICAL EVOLUTION

1. INTRODUCTION

In this chapter we analyse some of the unique features of GE using two problem domains described earlier in chapter 5, namely the Santa Fe ant trail and symbolic regression. In particular, our focus is turned to the wrapping operator and the degenerate genetic code.

Wrapping exists in GE mainly for the purpose of completion of an otherwise incomplete genotype-phenotype mapping. That is, in the event that the code being generated is still comprised of non-terminal symbols from the grammar, and the end of the genome has been reached, wrapping attempts to complete the mapping by allowing the re-use of the genome.

The degenerate genetic code is present in GE due to the modulo function that is adopted by the mapping function when selecting an appropriate production rule to be applied to the current non-terminal in the code being generated. We wish to establish if the degenerate genetic code could be playing a role in the maintenance of genetic diversity within our populations as has been observed in (Banzhaf, 1994). Kimura (Kimura, 1983) has claimed that neutral evolution is a candidate that could be responsible for the genetic diversity that is observed in biological populations, and could be enabled by virtue of the existence of the degenerate genetic code in GE. Recent findings suggest that the existence of a genetic code with a variable degree of degeneracy could allow a more efficient evolutionary search, resulting in greater fitness being attainable with higher degrees of degeneracy (Newman and Engelhardt, 1998).

A number of experiments are carried out to determine the utility and effects of the wrapping feature, and to elucidate whether the degenerate code is having an effect on the system's performance and genetic diversity. We firstly describe those experiments pertaining to the wrapping operator.

2. WRAPPING OPERATOR

Two sets of experiments for each problem domain are carried out with each test comprising 100 runs. In the first test the wrapping feature is enabled, and disabled in the second.

2.1 RESULTS

The results show that wrapping occurs, particularly in the earlier stages of runs, providing evidence that GE exploits this feature. The average number of individuals undergoing wrapping at each generation can be seen in Figure 6.1, and over time it can be seen that the number of individuals undergoing wrapping decreases.

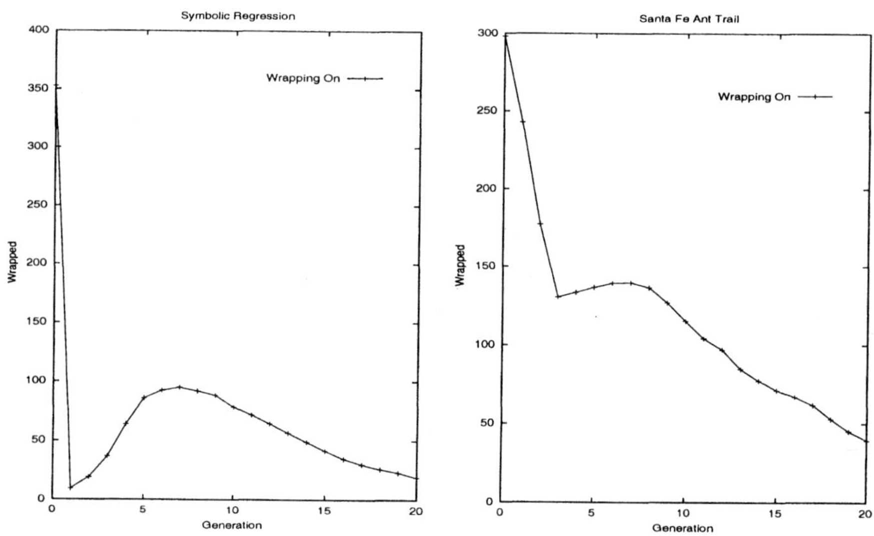

Figure 6.1. Number of individuals wrapped on the symbolic regression and Santa Fe trail problems.

2.1.1 INVALID INDIVIDUALS

Looking at the number of invalid individuals (Figure 6.2) we can see that there is a decrease in their numbers both in the presence and absence of wrapping over the initial generations. Recall that the simple initialisation scheme used by Grammatical Evolution generates random strings, without respect to syntactic validity, so the large numbers of invalid individuals in the initial generations isn't that surprising. Further, we can see from Figure 6.2 that, with wrapping, there are far fewer invalid individuals in the initial generations of the Santa Fe Ant Trail experiments than without, while for the Symbolic Regression problem, they are virtually identical. This suggests that wrapping is less important for the Symbolic Regression problem.

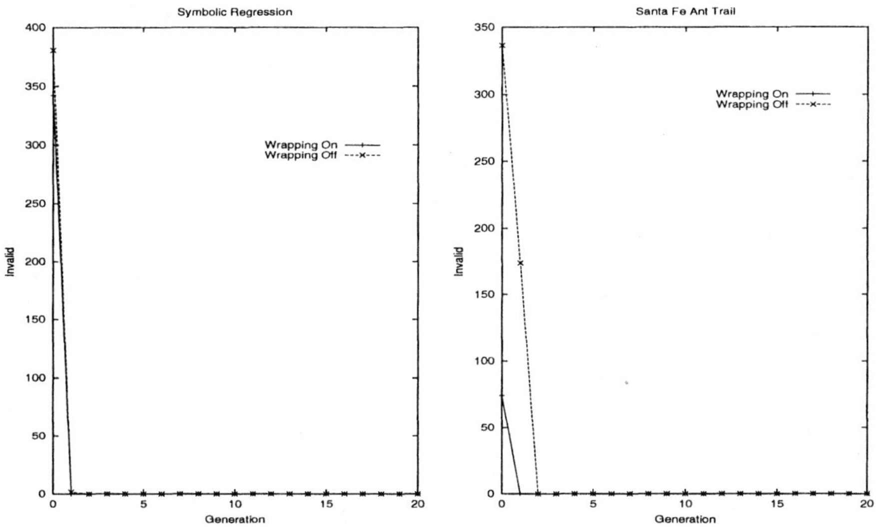

Figure 6.2. The number of invalid individuals for each generation in the presence and absence of wrapping on the symbolic regression and Santa Fe trail problems. This figures illustrates that all invalid individuals are removed from the population early on in runs, even without wrapping being present, due to the replacement mechanism.

2.1.2 CUMULATIVE FREQUENCY OF SUCCESS

The effect of wrapping or otherwise on the cumulative frequency of success measures can be seen in Figure 6.3. As can be seen, there appears to be no effect on the success rates on the symbolic regression problem. However, in the case of the Santa Fe trail, there is a decrease in the cumulative frequency of success when wrapping is disabled.

2.1.3 GENOME LENGTHS

A comparison of the average actual genome lengths to the average effective genome lengths is given in Figure 6.4. The effective genome length is a measure of the number of expressed genes during the genotype-to-phenotype mapping process, while the actual length is the number of genes on the chromosome. The actual length is, on average, longer than the effective length for these problems, and when wrapping is turned off the actual genome lengths increase on the symbolic regression problem.

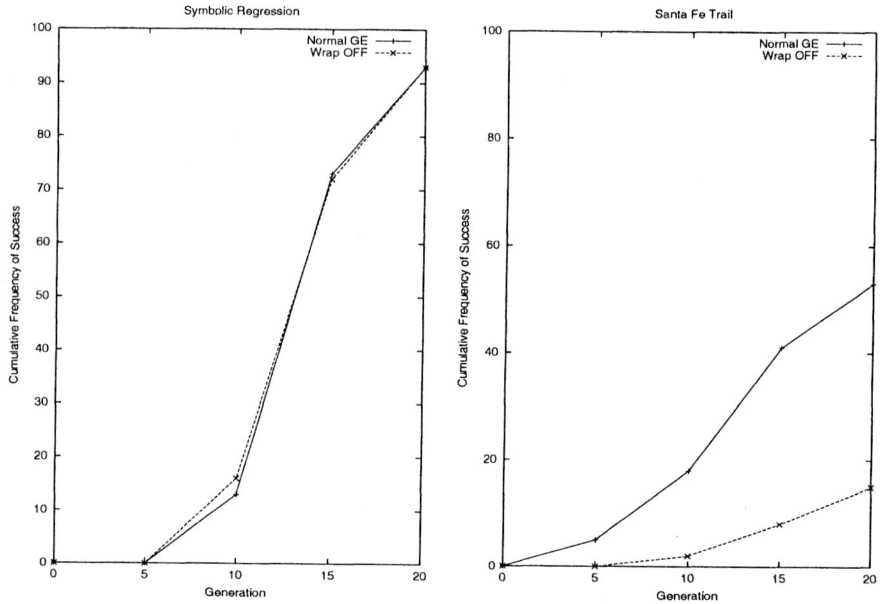

Figure 6.3. Figure shows the cumulative frequency of success measures on both problems with and without the presence of wrapping.

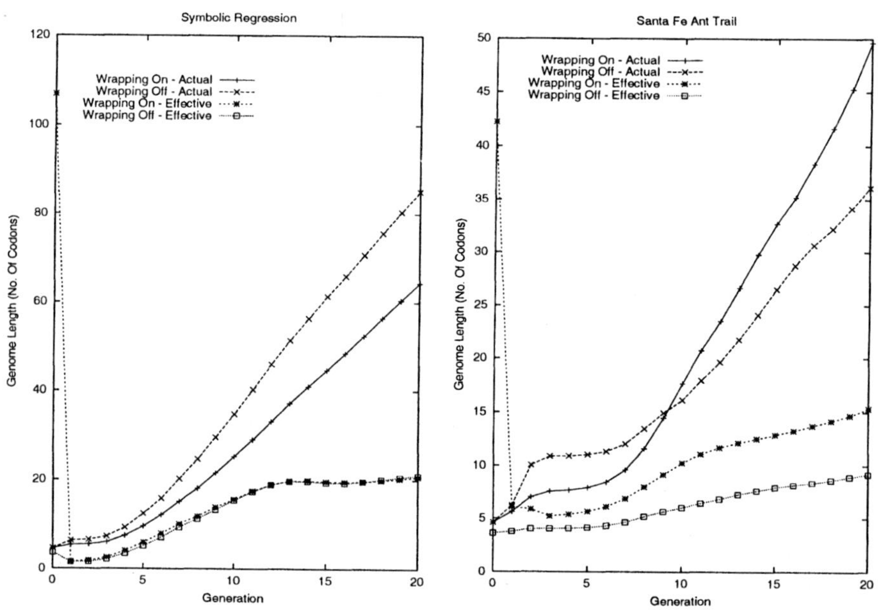

Figure 6.4. The figure shows the actual versus effective genome length for symbolic regression and the Santa Fe trail in the presence and absence of wrapping.

On the Santa Fe trail problem, the actual lengths increase initially when compared to the values in the absence of wrapping, but as time progresses the actual genome lengths are greater in the presence of wrapping.

For symbolic regression, this illustrates that the wrapping mechanism reuses the codons that are already present on the genome, in effect compressing the program into a smaller number of codons rather than extending its physical length.

2.2 DISCUSSION

In the symbolic regression problem it is noted that while genome lengths are constrained when the wrapping feature is enabled, there is little effect on the cumulative frequency of success.

The fact that the wrapping feature is important to finding solutions to the Santa Fe trail in 20 generations, and no ill effects are demonstrated in performance on the symbolic regression problem when wrapping is disabled, suggests that wrapping is a useful feature to have available and, at the very least, doesn't harm solutions.

The dependency of the Santa Fe trail's solution success rate on wrapping can be attributed to the regular, repetitive nature of the required solution that can be exploited effectively by the wrapping mechanism, particularly earlier on in runs. Solutions are comprised of sequences of the operations $left()$, $right()$, and $move()$ with some conditional statements that allow the ant to search for the next piece of food. This search can be achieved through a repetitive application of these operators.

A comparison of the number of invalid individuals produced in both problem domains examined here shows that invalid individuals are restricted almost exclusively to the initial generations (Figure 6.2). The effective removal of these unwanted individuals could be attributed to the selection and replacement mechanisms used in these experiments, in particular the steady state replacement strategy. This is an example of the effective use of the illegal individual replacement constraint (i.e. the removal of incompletely mapped individuals in the case of GE) to evolve legal phenotypes, as described in (Yu and Bentley, 1998). The effective operation of GE is not dependent, however, on using a steady state replacement strategy.

In summary, wrapping is shown to be useful in improving the success rate of runs, and is also responsible for constraining genome lengths.

3. DEGENERATE GENETIC CODE

In this case six sets of experiments are carried out for each problem domain. The first set comprises 100 runs in which genetic code degeneracy is removed as far as possible by reducing the number of bits in a codon to the lowest possible value that can still represent the maximum number of productions rules belonging to any one non-terminal. The second set is of another 100 runs in which degeneracy is present as in the standard GE implementation using 8-bit codons (O'Neill and Ryan, 1999b).

The third set of 100 runs consider the situation where the degeneracy is increased above the standard GE implementation, in this case with the adoption of 16-bit codons.

In addition, a fourth, fifth and sixth set of runs are conducted to take into consideration degrees of degeneracy between 16 and 8-bits (12-bits), and between 8-bits and the case where degeneracy is removed (6-bits, and 4-bits).

In the standard GE implementation each codon can represent 256 distinct integer values. Therefore, in this state GE can represent up to 256 productions for each non-terminal in the grammar. In the case of the Santa Fe trail the maximum number of productions that any one non-terminal has is 3, and for symbolic regression problems this number is 4. As a result, the minimum number of bits any codon can have in the case of these problems is two, as this can represent a maximum of 4 distinct productions. It follows that in the case of the symbolic regression problem, all degeneracy has been removed, while it still exists to a small extent in the Santa Fe trail problem.

We wish to examine the effects that the degenerate code has on the genetic diversity in our population, and we do this by examined two measures of diversity. The first is termed the *mean variety* and is obtained by calculating the average of the variances at each bit locus on the genome, and is given by the following formula:

$$Mean\ Variety = \frac{\sum_{1}^{L} \frac{\sum_{i=1}^{N} (X_i - \mu)^2}{N}}{L}$$

where X_i is the locus value at position i, μ is the mean of X_i at locus i, N is the sample population size, and L is the number of loci analysed.

With a population size of 500, the maximum mean variety value obtainable is 0.25. The value 0.25 corresponds to those populations with a greater degree of variance, whereas those populations with values tending towards zero have lower degrees of variance. This measure attempts to establish how different the individual genotypes in any given population are. The second measure of variety is simply the number of unique individuals in a population, and can be used to some extent to illustrate the genetic diversity within a population (Langdon, 1998).

3.1 RESULTS

A cumulative frequency measure in the presence and absence of code degeneracy can be seen in Figure 6.5 that shows a superior performance on the Santa Fe trail in the presence of a degenerate code. The difference in the case of the easier symbolic regression problem is not as clear, indeed both 12 and 16-bit do not perform as well as when degeneracy is switched off.

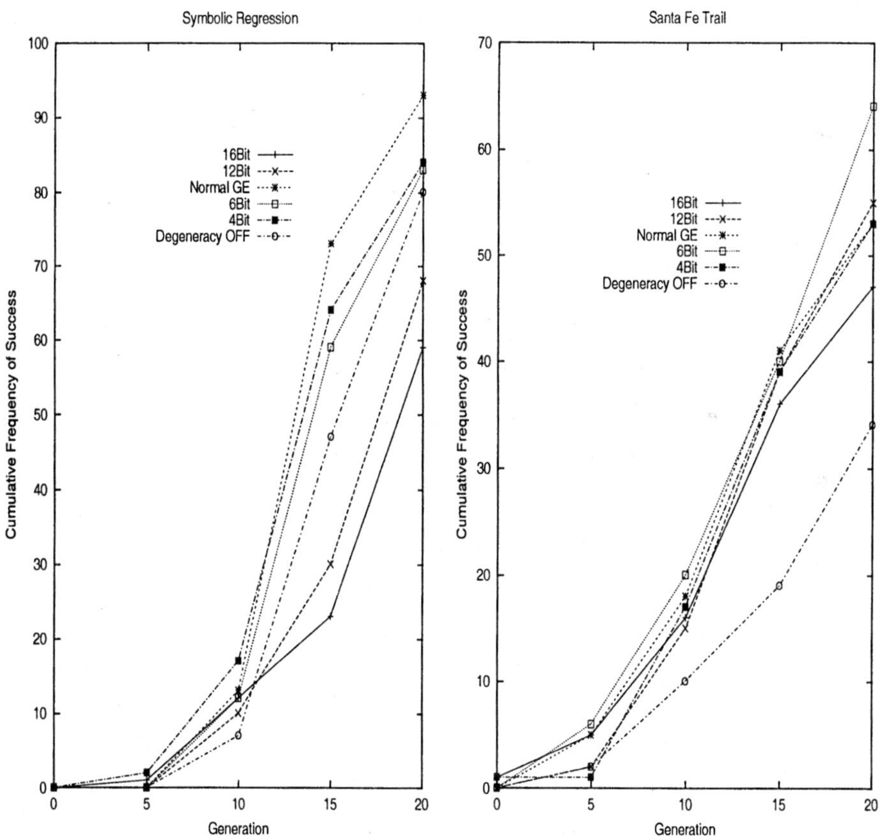

Figure 6.5. Cumulative frequencies of success for both problem domains in the presence and absence of genetic code degeneracy.

It would appear that increasing the number of bits in a codon to 16 on the symbolic regression problem resulted in slower evolutionary times. To test this we re-ran the 8, 12 and 16-bit experiments on both problems for 50 generations, and the results can be seen in Figure 6.6. The cumulative frequencies of success demonstrate the slower evolutionary times involved with the 12 and 16-bit

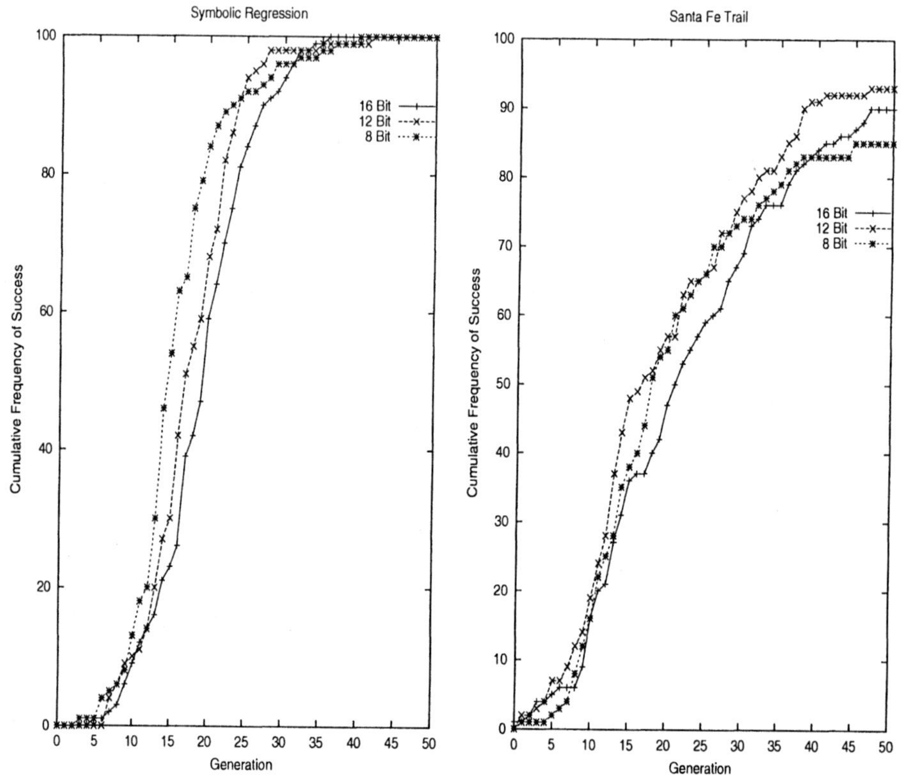

Figure 6.6. Cumulative frequencies of success for both problem domains in the presence and absence of genetic code degeneracy over 50 generations.

codons, whereupon approaching 50 generations the 12 and 16-bit surpasses the 8-bit encoding on both problems.

3.1.1 DIVERSITY MEASURES

The genotypic diversity measures are carried out for the 100 runs. The average of these values for each generation over all the runs can be seen in Figures 6.7 and 6.8. These graphs show that the code degeneracy has a marked effect on the mean variety measure and on the number of unique individuals. In the case where the degenerate code is removed there is a clear decrease in the mean variety and in the number of unique individuals at each generation. This suggests that the degenerate code plays a role in maintaining genetic diversity within the population.

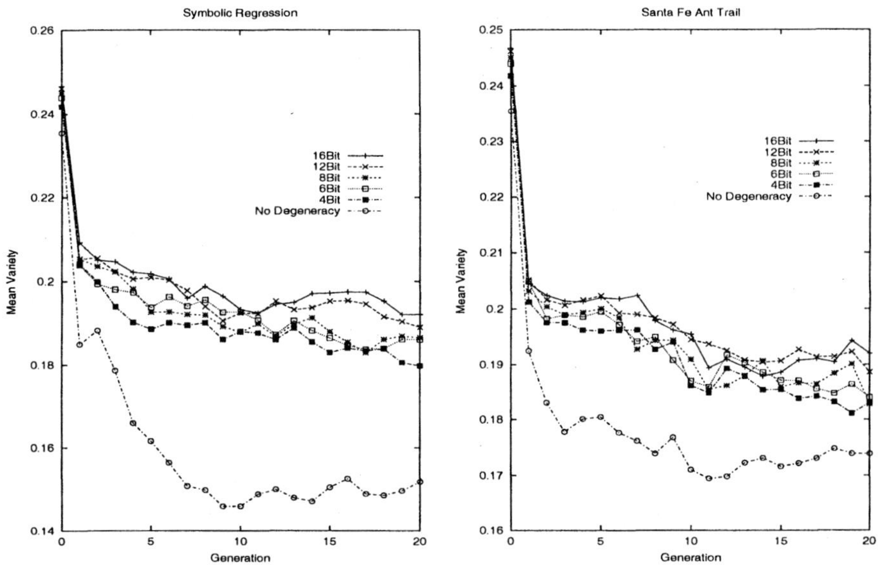

Figure 6.7. The figure shows the genetic code degeneracy and mean variety on symbolic regression and Santa Fe trail problems.

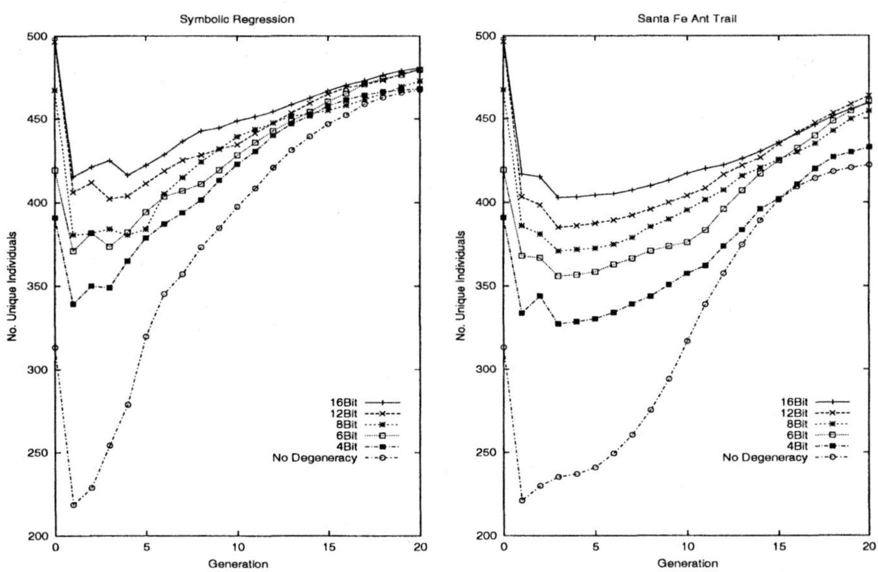

Figure 6.8. The figure shows genetic code degeneracy and unique individuals (for actual genome) on both problem domains.

3.2 DISCUSSION

Based on the two measures used to give an indication of the genotypic diversity in a population, the results show that degeneracy in the genetic code has a beneficial effect on genotypic diversity in the population.

The fact that GE is capable of maintaining genetic diversity throughout a run could prove to be a very useful feature if the system was to be applied to problems that required an adaptive property, such as dynamic problem domains.

As well as the benefits noted for genetic diversity, the cumulative frequencies of success (Figure 6.5) show that the degenerate code improves the performance of the system in terms of its success rate at finding solutions on the more difficult Santa Fe trail problem. The results suggest that the adoption of degeneracy in GE should have positive effects on the systems performance, but, depending on the amount of degeneracy incorporated, slower evolutionary times may result. For the problem domains examined here, with a maximum number of choices of four productions rules for any one non-terminal in the grammar, a codon of 6 to 8-bits appears appropriate (i.e., an average of 32 genetic codes representing any one production rule). However, when one is trying to solve a real world problem, the time taken is often less important than the quality of the solution eventually discovered, so it is possible that, on more difficult problems, a higher level may be useful.

To summarise, the degenerate code maintains genetic diversity, and improves the performance of the system in terms of the success rate of runs. As the adoption of 8-bit codons produces consistent results across the problems analysed here, we recommend the use of this codon size. It must be noted, however, that we do not expect this codon size to be the optimal across all problems, indeed it may not be the optimal for the problem domains examined here. As such, an investigation into more appropriate codon sizes may be beneficial.

Results in (Miller and Thomson, 2000) also show an improvement in performance on the Santa Fe trail problem in the presence of large redundancy in the genotype representation.

4. REMOVAL OF WRAPPING AND DEGENERACY

A further set of experiments was conducted to determine the effects of removing both wrapping and degeneracydegenerate genetic code. Over 100 runs, on both problem domains, this set examines the cumulative frequency of success, genome lengths, and the genetic diversity measures.

4.1 RESULTS

Figure 6.9 shows the cumulative frequency of success for the case where both wrapping and degeneracy are removed, a comparison to when both are present as in standard GE, the cases where only wrapping is switched off, and degeneracy alone is removed.

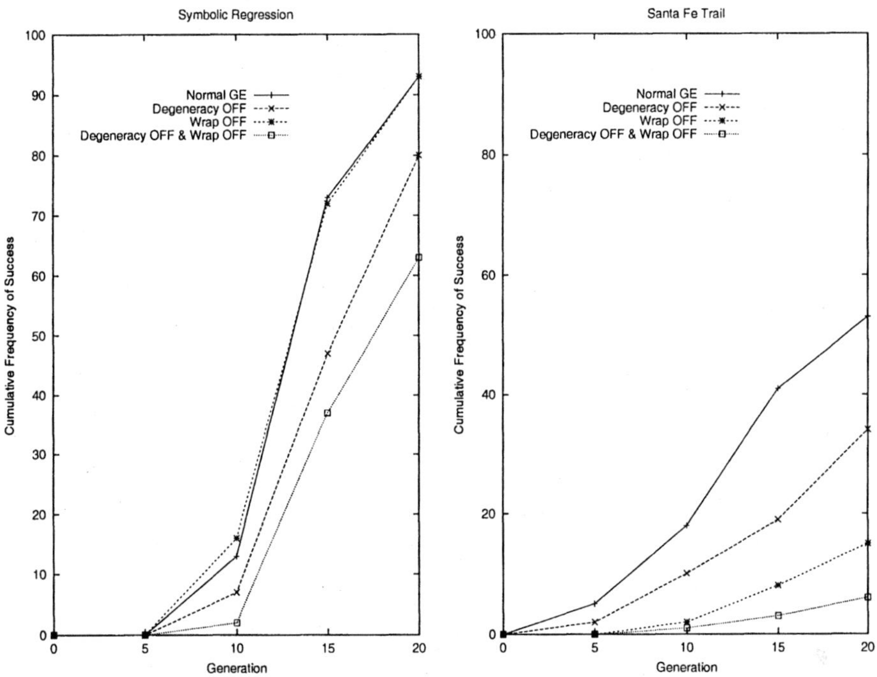

Figure 6.9. A comparison of the cumulative frequency of success on the Santa Fe trail and symbolic regression with the removal of wrapping and degeneracy, against the cases where both are present, and where each is removed individually.

We can clearly see a degradation of performance, in terms of the success rates of finding solutions, in these graphs, with the worst performance occurring when both wrapping and degeneracy are removed. Notice that, in the case of Symbolic Regression, while turning off wrapping alone (as indicated in section 2.1.3) has virtually no effect on the performance, it has a significant effect when degeneracy is turned off, indicating that, even in this case, the two phenomena have a cumulative effect.

Examining the genome lengths (Figure 6.10), in the case of the symbolic regression problem, we see an increase in the actual lengths as we remove each feature, until we get the largest increases when both wrapping and degeneracy are removed. On the Santa Fe trail genome lengths are considerably shorter than for symbolic regression with the trend not being as clear in this case. With wrapping switched off, and when both wrapping and degeneracy are off, we see a slight decrease in average genome lengths in the order of 5% after 20 generations. When compared with the symbolic regression results, differences

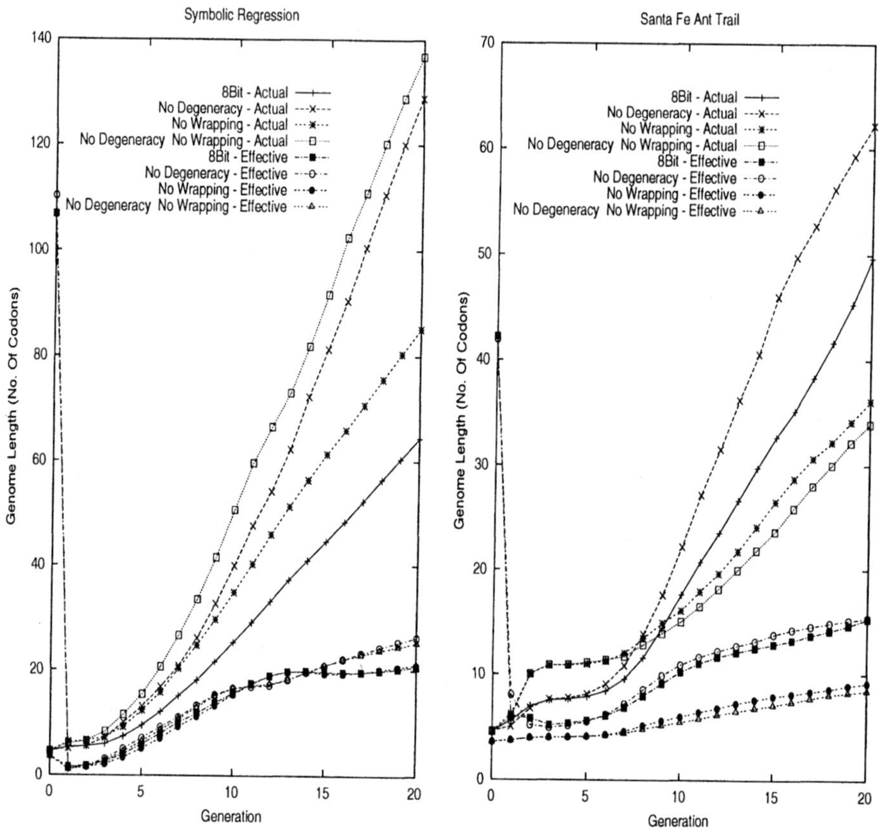

Figure 6.10. A comparison of genome lengths on both problems, with the removal of wrapping and degeneracy, against the cases where both are present, and where each is removed individually.

in the order of 62% occur when both wrapping and degeneracy are switched off. As genome lengths do not have a detrimental affect with the presence of wrapping and degeneracy on the Santa Fe trail, and are clearly beneficial in the case of symbolic regression, their continued use by GE is justified.

With respect to the genetic diversity measures we would not expect to see a further degradation in diversity with the absence of both wrapping and degeneracy, and this is illustrated in Figures 6.11 and 6.12.

5. MUTATION RATES

A final set of experiments was conducted to investigate the possibility that an implicit change in mutation rates could be responsible for the performance effects observed with the degeneracy experiments. By removing degeneracy we reduce the number of bits in a codon, and as such we effectively reduce the

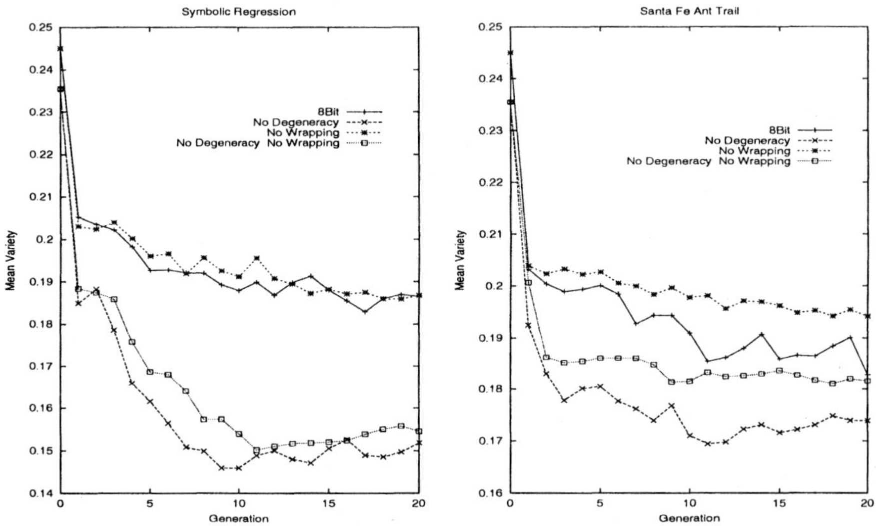

Figure 6.11. A comparison of the mean variety measure on both problems, with the removal of wrapping and degeneracy, against the cases where both are present, and where each is removed individually.

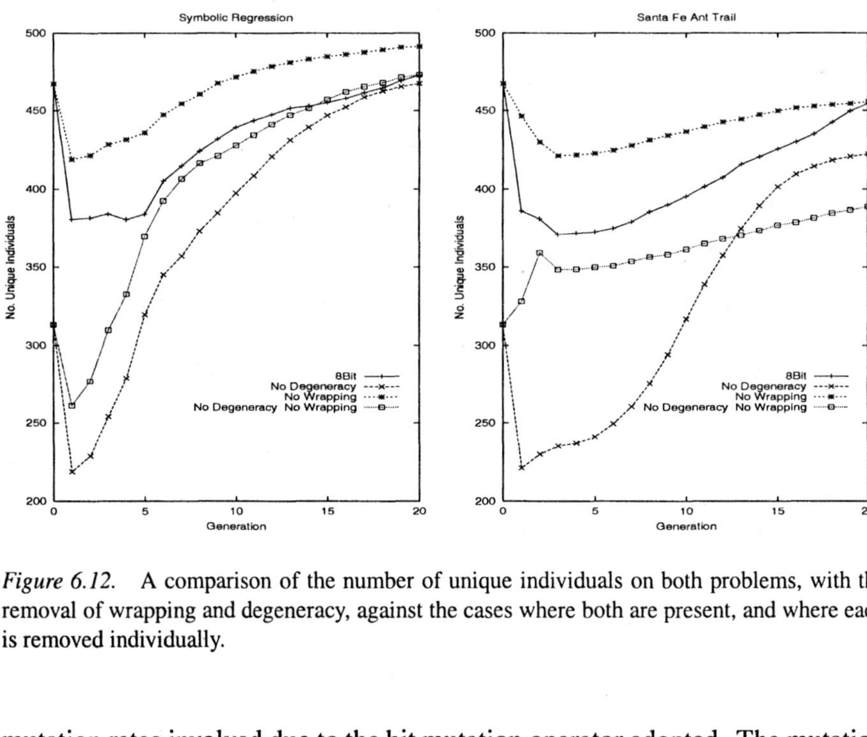

Figure 6.12. A comparison of the number of unique individuals on both problems, with the removal of wrapping and degeneracy, against the cases where both are present, and where each is removed individually.

mutation rates involved due to the bit mutation operator adopted. The mutation operator acts by testing each bit locus of a genome and mutating each with a pre-specified probability.

We conducted experiments whereby the mutation rate for the standard GE implementation with 8-bit codons is decreased to 0.001 from 0.01, and where the mutation rate in the case of the removal of degeneracy is increased proportionately to the new smaller codon size, to 0.0333. These results can then be compared to the standard and smaller codon size results with the usual mutation rate of 0.01.

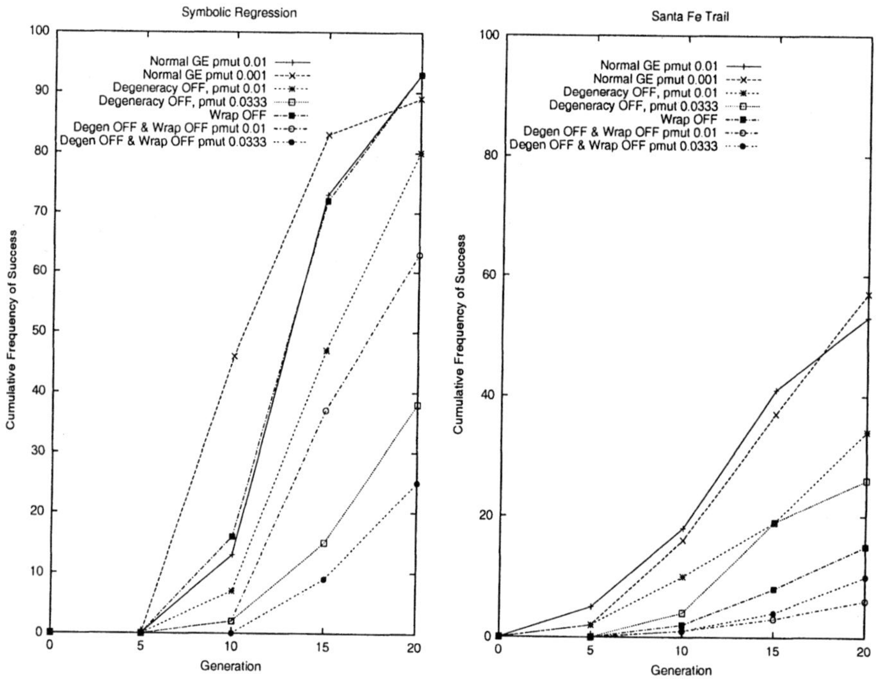

Figure 6.13. A cumulative frequency of success on symbolic regression and the Santa Fe trail with scaled mutation rates.

5.1 RESULTS

Figure 6.13 illustrates the results for these experiments on the cumulative frequency of success for both problem domains. For symbolic regression, when degeneracy is removed and the mutation rate is increased, we see a further degradation in performance. Clearly, the increased mutation rate has a disruptive effect on the evolutionary search due to the lack of degeneracy. On the Santa Fe trail problem, the cumulative frequencies are generally insensitive to the mutation rate adopted for the parameters examined here. The results demonstrate that the degeneracy effects observed are largely as a result of the degenerate genetic code employed by GE and not an artifact of a mutation rate change.

6. CONCLUSIONS

The effects of the wrapping operator and the degenerate genetic code have been investigated in GE. We have demonstrated the utility of the wrapping operator. We have also observed that wrapping can result in the compression of genotypic lengths. On the Santa Fe trail problem it was observed that wrapping clearly improved the success rate of GE. With respect to the degenerate genetic code we have illustrated the many benefits that this feature confers on GE, i.e. an improvement in success rate on both problem domains examined, and maintenance in genetic diversity of the population, when a degenerate genetic code is used. When both features were removed from GE, we subsequently observed a further degradation in the system's performance. Clearly, both wrapping and the degenerate genetic code play an important role in GE, at worst they have no ill effects on any of the problems examined, and at best they can improve performance. In the next chapter we go on to analyse crossover in GE.

Chapter 7

CROSSOVER IN GRAMMATICAL EVOLUTION

1. INTRODUCTION

While crossover is generally accepted as an explorative operator in string based G.A.s (Goldberg, 1989), the benefit or otherwise of employing crossover in tree based Genetic Programming is often disputed. Work such as (Collins, 1992) went as far as to dismiss GP as a biological search method due to its use of trees, while (Angeline, 1997) presented results which suggested that crossover in GP can provide little benefit over randomly generating subtrees.

GE utilises linear genomes and, as with GP systems, has come under fire for its seemingly destructive crossover operator, a simple one-point crossover inspired from GA's. In this chapter we address crossover in GE, seeking answers to the question of how destructive our one-point crossover operator is, and to establish if the system could benefit from a biologically inspired crossover (O'Neill et al., 2003).

By default, GE employs a standard GA variable length, one-point crossover operator as follows: (i) Two crossover points are selected at random, one on each individual (ii) The segments on the right hand side of each individual are then swapped.

Other researchers have proposed a number of novel crossover operators (Francone et al., 1999; Langdon, 1999; Langdon, 2000). Each of Langdon and Francone et al. derived different homologous crossover operators, the former on tree based GP and the latter on linear structures, being introduced to improve exploration (Francone et al., 1999; Langdon, 1999).

Both of these works exploit the idea of a homologous crossover operation, which draws inspiration from the molecular biological crossover process. The principle being exploited is the fact that in nature the entities swapping genetic material only swap fragments that belong to the same position and are of similar size. This, it has been proposed, results in more productive crossover events. Indeed, results from both Langdon and Francone et al. provide evidence in support of this claim.

The homologous crossover operator applied to linear genomes in (Francone et al., 1999) is called *Sticky Crossover*, and operates by swapping instructions at the same locus. It makes no attempt to swap functionally equivalent code segments. In the tree-based homologous crossover (Langdon, 2000) the crossover point on the first parent is selected as normal in GP. The crossover point on the second parent is determined by taking into account the size of the subtree created from the first crossover point, and selecting the subtree in the second parent that is closest to it. Closeness is measured by looking at the tree shapes, and at the distance between the two crossover points and the root nodes of the individuals.

A consequence of these conservative crossover operators is a reduction in the bloat phenomenon, which is due, at least in part, to the fact that these new operators are less destructive. Bloat is a phenomenon whereby the sizes of individuals in a GP population increase dramatically over the duration of a run, largely due to redundant code. Suggestions have been made that destructive crossover events could be responsible for bloat; bloat arises as a mechanism to prevent destructive crossover events occurring by acting as buffering regions in which crossover can occur without harming functionality. The emergence of increasingly longer genomes is, therefore, less likely with less destructive crossover.

As with many non-binary representations, it is often not clear how much useful genetic material is being exchanged during crossover, and thus not clear how much exploration is actually taking place.

The chapter begins with an investigation into a novel biologically-inspired, homologous crossover operator for GE. Following on from the disappointing results for the homologous operator experiments we conduct an analysis of the effectiveness of the simple one-point crossover operator by switching the operator off, and by using a headless chicken crossover. This set of experiments is designed to test the hypothesis that the one-point operator is acting in a productive fashion with the exchange of useful building blocks. Finally, the mechanism of crossover in GE is discussed providing insights into the type of fragments exchanged during crossover, and the manner in which these fragments are exchanged. Consequently the one-point operator is dubbed ripple crossover due to its effects on the derivation trees.

2. HOMOLOGOUS CROSSOVER

This section serves to initiate our investigation of crossover in GE, and proposes a new form of operator inspired by molecular biology and the novel homologous crossover operators designed for GP. We compare the standard GE one point crossover to two different versions of this homologous crossover, as well as two alternative forms of a two-point crossover operator.

The standard GE homologous crossover proceeds as follows:

1 During the mapping process a history of the rules selected in the grammar are stored for each individual.

2 The histories of the two individuals to crossover are aligned.

3 Each history is read sequentially from the left while the rules selected are identical for both individuals, this region of similarity is noted.

4 The first two crossover points are selected to be at the boundary of the region of similarity, these points are the same on both individuals.

5 The two second crossover points are then selected randomly from the regions of dissimilarity.

6 A two-point crossover is then performed.

An outline of this operator can be seen in Figure 7.1.

The reasoning behind this operator is the facilitation of the recombination of blocks that are in context with respect to the current state of the mapping process. In this case these blocks are of differing lengths.

The second form of the homologous crossover operator differs only in that it swaps blocks of identical size. In step 5, the two, second crossover points are at the same locus on each individual.

The two-point crossover operators employed are the standard GA two-point operator (fragments of unequal size), and one in which the size of the fragments being swapped are the same.

2.1 EXPERIMENTAL APPROACH

For each type of crossover, 100 runs were carried out on the Santa Fe ant trail and Symbolic regression problems, as described in chapter 5. Performance of each operator was measured in terms of each of the following

1 Cumulative frequency of success

2 Average size of fragments being swapped at each generation

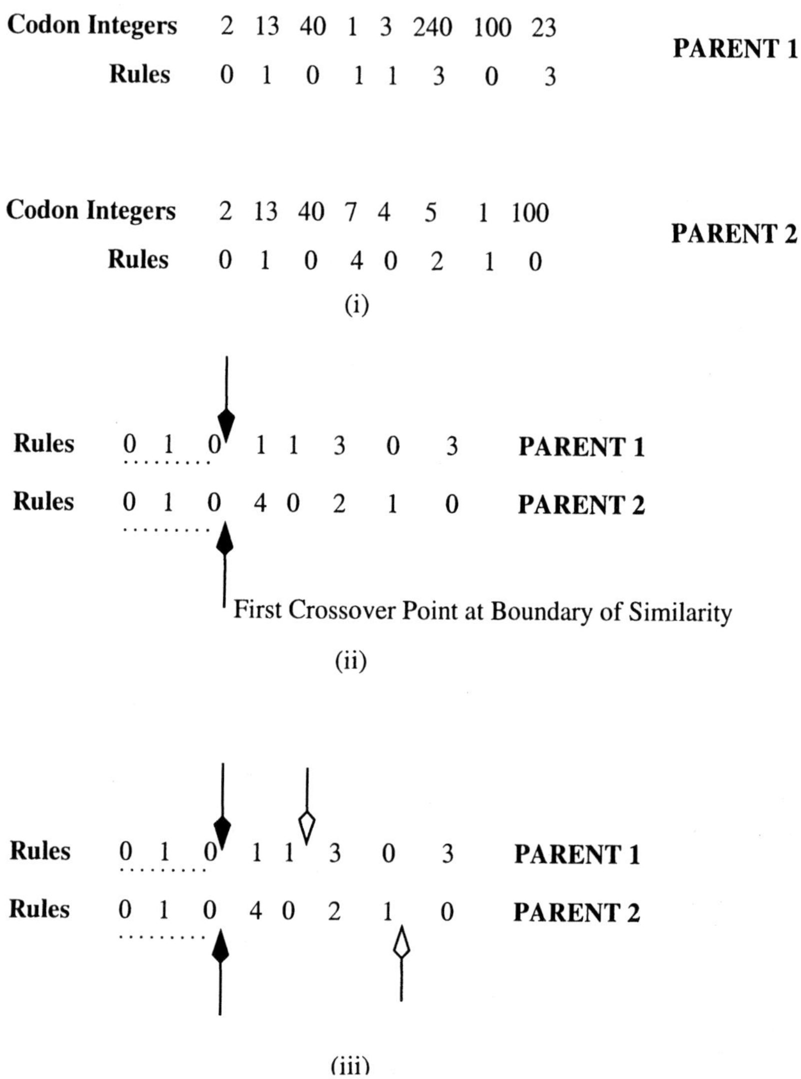

Figure 7.1. Standard GE homologous crossover. (i) Shows two parents represented as their codon integer values on top, and the corresponding rules selected during the mapping process below each integer value. (ii) The rule strings (mapping histories) are aligned, and the region of similarity noted (underlined). The first crossover points are selected at this boundary. (iii) The second crossover points are then selected after the boundary of similarity for each individual.

3 Ratio of the average fragment size being swapped to the average genome length

4 Ratio of crossover events resulting in successful propagation of the individual to the next generation and the total number of crossover events.

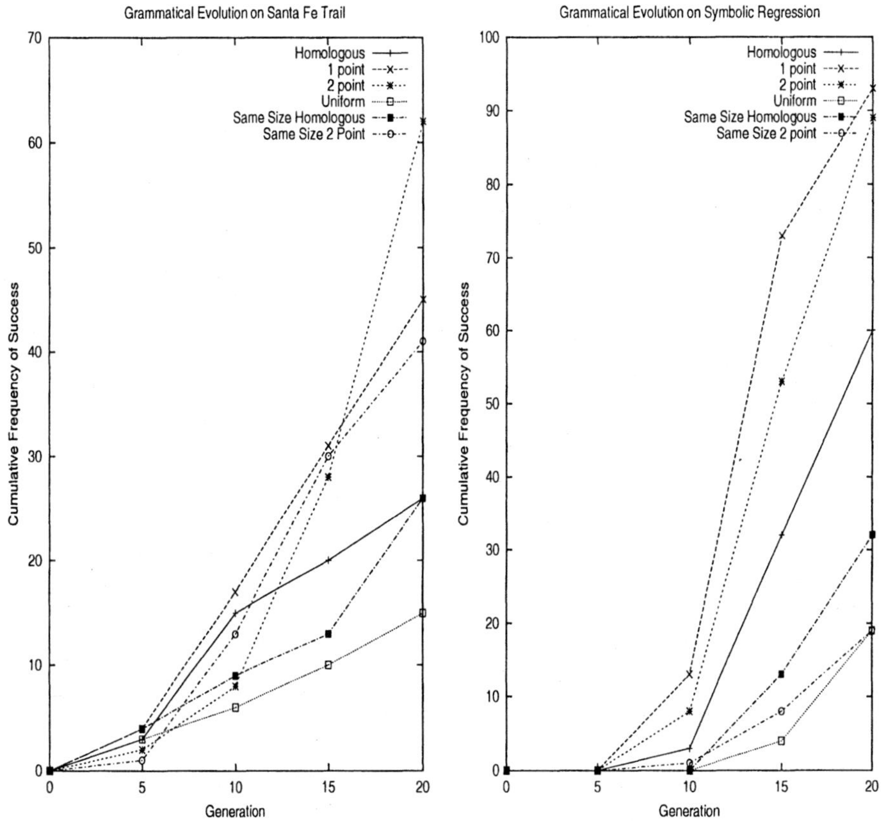

Figure 7.2. Comparison of the cumulative frequencies of success for each crossover operator on the Santa Fe ant trail and symbolic regression problems.

Measures (2) and (3) have been used previously in (Poli and Langdon, 1998). Measure (4) is used to determine the productiveness of the crossover operator by looking at the number of individuals that are propagated to the next generation after having undergone crossover. Tableaus describing the parameters and terminals are given in chapter 5.

2.2 RESULTS

As can be seen in Figure 7.2, the cumulative frequencies of success clearly show that standard one and two point crossover are superior to the other operators on both problem domains. We will now describe the results for each operator under the other measures described in the previous section.

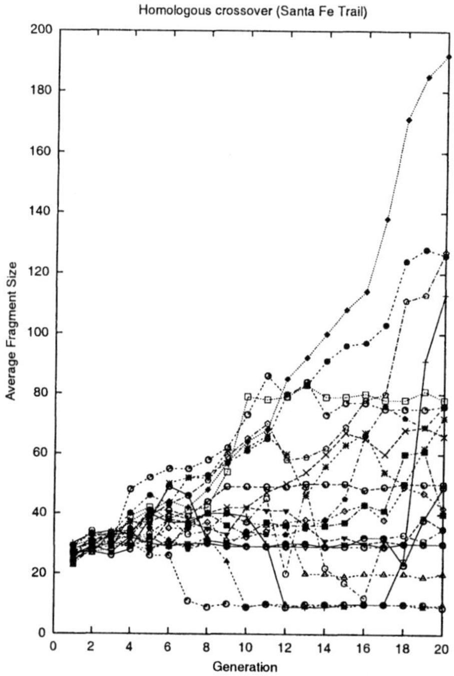

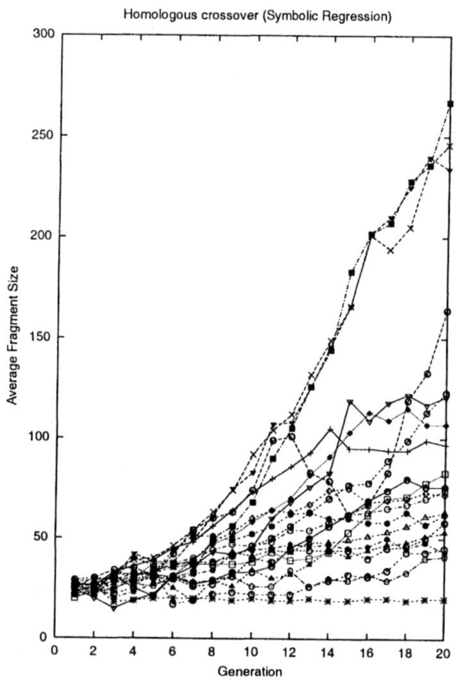

Figure 7.3. Average fragment size being swapped each generation for Homologous crossover

Figure 7.3 shows the average fragment size being swapped at each generation with homologous crossover. Data is presented for 20 separate runs and plotted in this manner because we are interested in general trends over the set of runs as opposed to the precise details for individual runs in each of these graphs.

Overall the fragment size increases as each generation passes, although the lengths of the chromosomes are also increasing. As such, it is difficult to see what is happening to the fragment size. A more useful measure of the ratio of average fragment size to the average chromosome length can be seen in Figure 7.4.

Similar graphs for same size homologous, two point, same size two point, and one point can be seen in Figures 7.5, 7.6, 7.7, and 7.8, respectively.

For each of the homologous crossover operators and the one point operator, on average 50% of the genetic material is being exchanged during these events. This suggests that these operators can act as global search operators *throughout* a run.

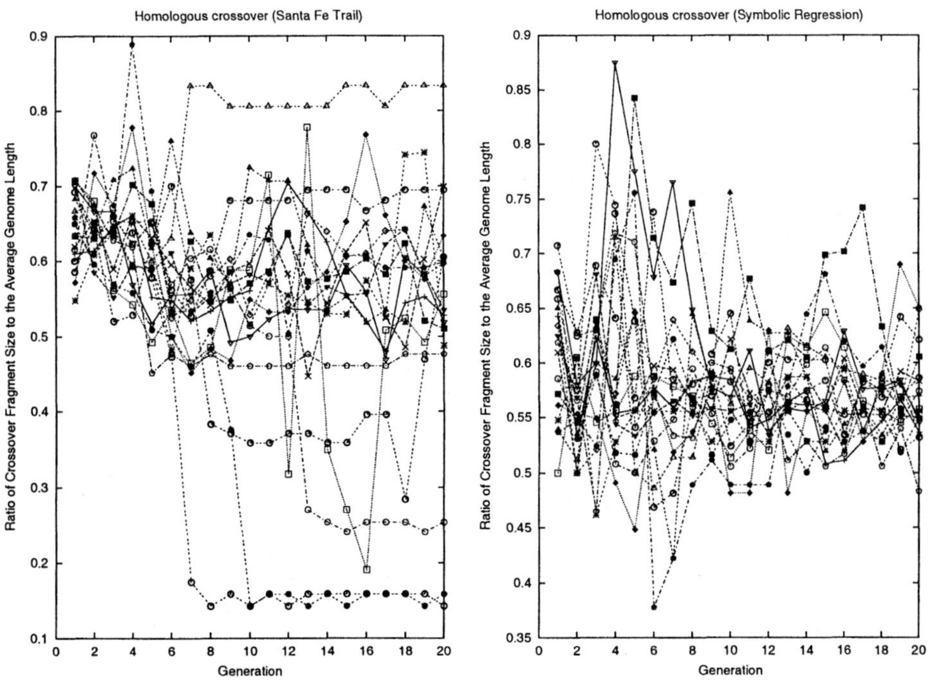

Figure 7.4. Ratio (centered around 0.6) of the average fragment size being swapped and the average chromosome length at each generation for Homologous crossover

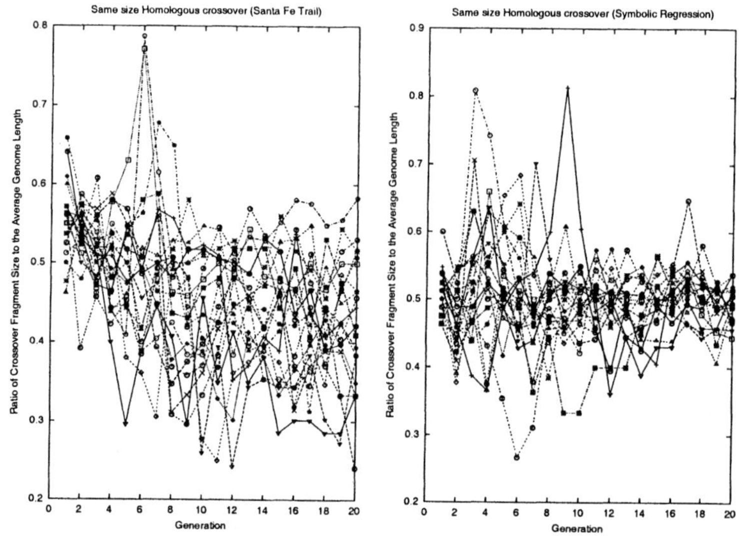

Figure 7.5. Ratio (centered around 0.5) of the average fragment size being swapped and the average chromosome length at each generation for Same size Homologous crossover

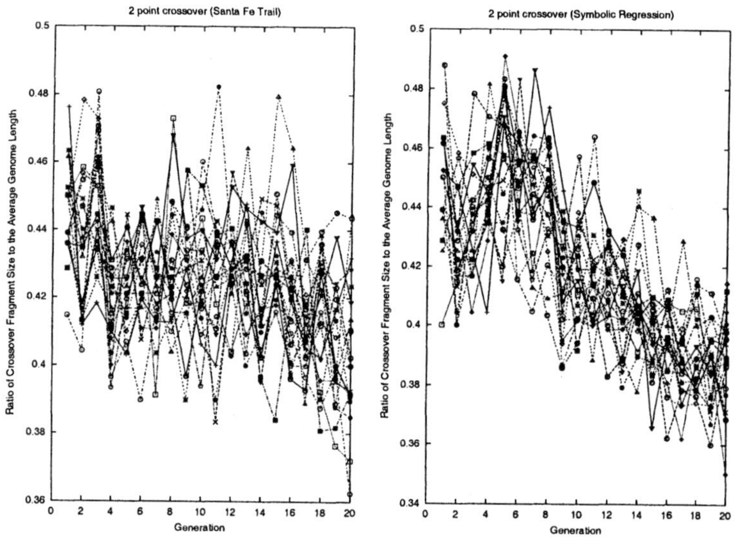

Figure 7.6. Ratio (centered around 0.43) of the average fragment size being swapped and the average chromosome length at each generation for two point crossover

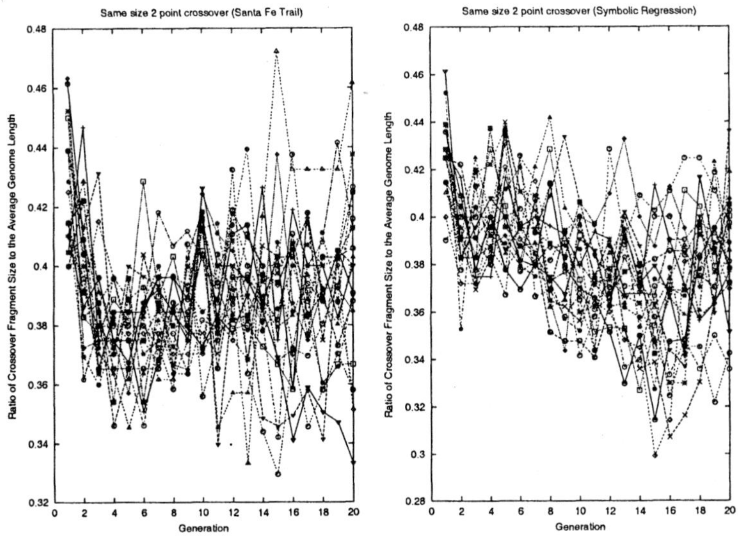

Figure 7.7. Ratio (centered around 0.4) of the average fragment size being swapped and the average chromosome length at each generation for same size two point crossover

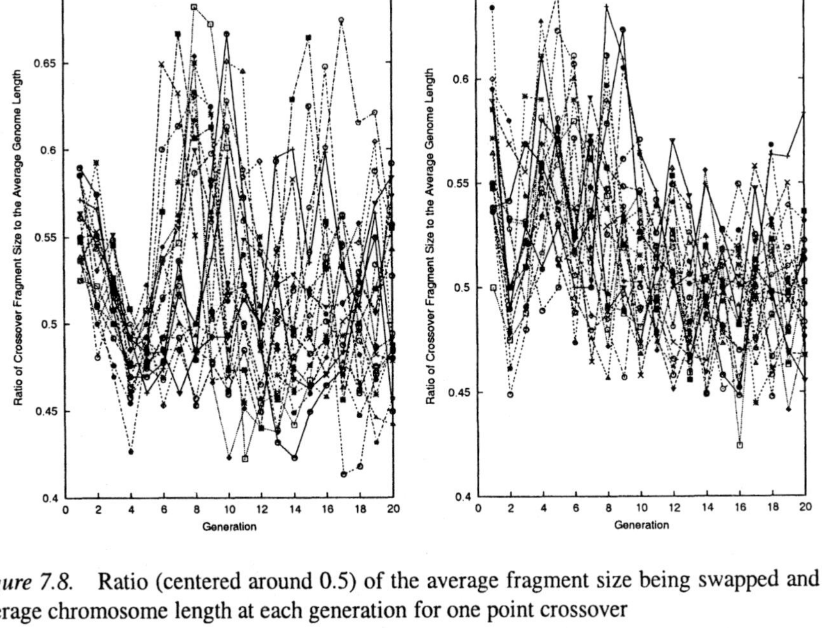

Figure 7.8. Ratio (centered around 0.5) of the average fragment size being swapped and the average chromosome length at each generation for one point crossover

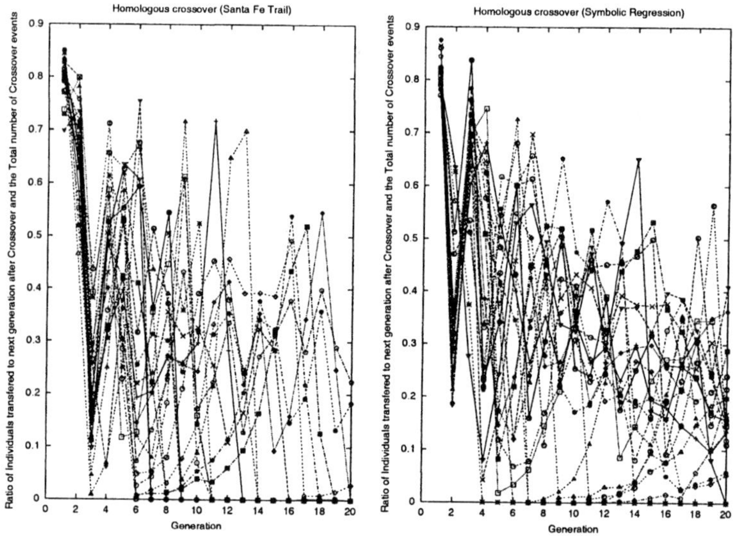

Figure 7.9. Ratio of the number of individuals undergoing Homologous crossover that have been propagated to the next generation and the total number of crossover events occurring in that generation.

Figure 7.9 shows the ratio of individuals undergoing crossover that have been successfully propagated to the next generation and the total number of crossover events that have occurred. The results of this measure for all other operators can be seen in Figures 7.10, 7.11, 7.12, and 7.13. For both homologous operators there is no obvious trend to the data, indeed, the transmission of individuals as a result of homologous crossover to the next generation would appear to be erratic. Both of the two point operators and the one point crossover each have clearer trends. The two-point operator does appear to be less successful on this measure. On the Santa Fe trail, propagation is more erratic than on the symbolic regression problem. We propose this is as a result of the dependency on the use of the wrapping operator that would have an effect of making crossover more disruptive.

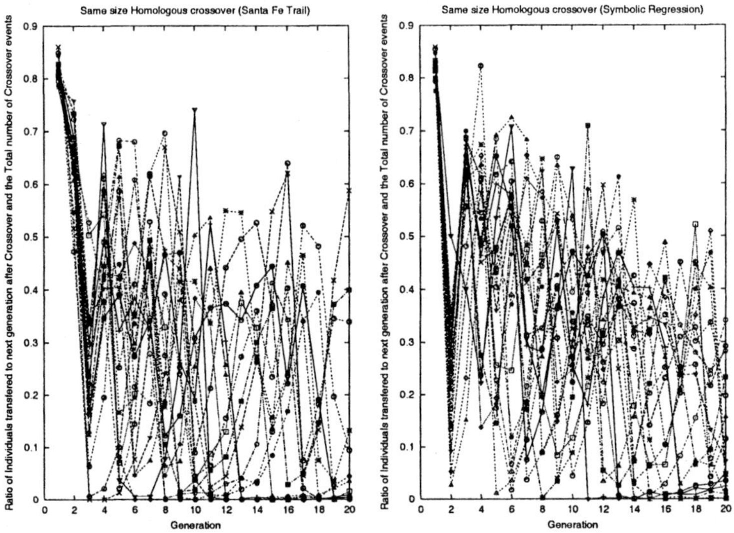

Figure 7.10. Ratio of the number of individuals undergoing Same size Homologous crossover that have been propagated to the next generation and the total number of crossover events occurring in that generation.

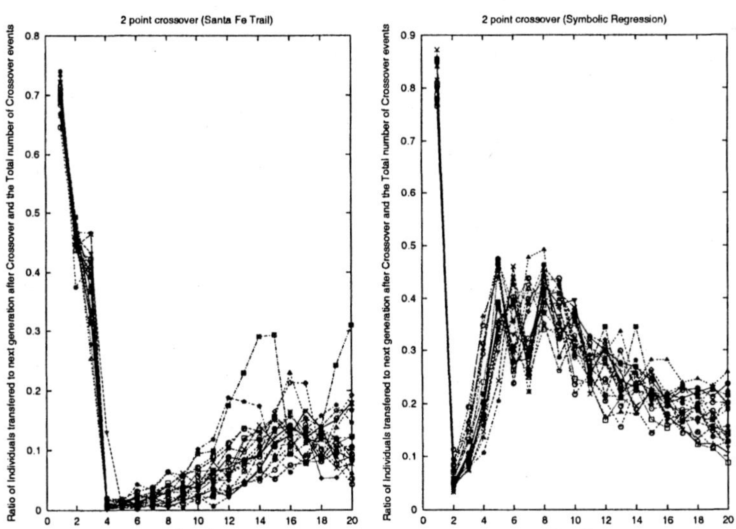

Figure 7.11. Ratio of the number of individuals undergoing two point crossover that have been propagated to the next generation and the total number of crossover events occurring in that generation.

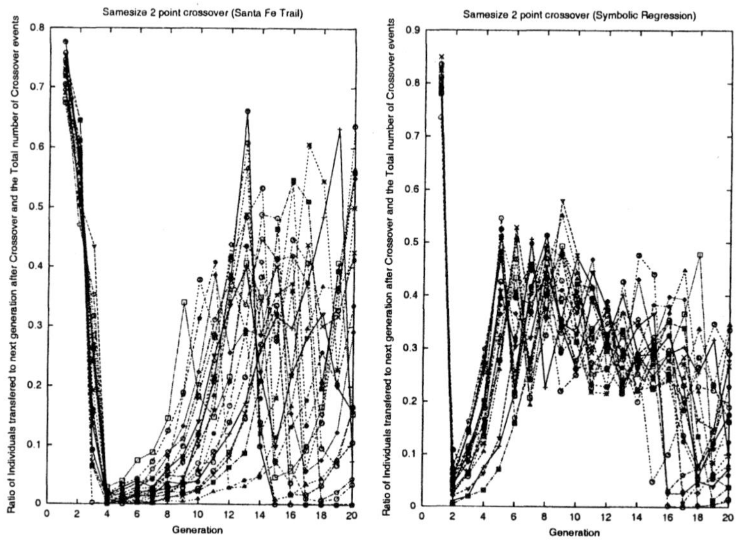

Figure 7.12. Ratio of the number of individuals undergoing same size two point crossover that have been propagated to the next generation and the total number of crossover events occurring in that generation.

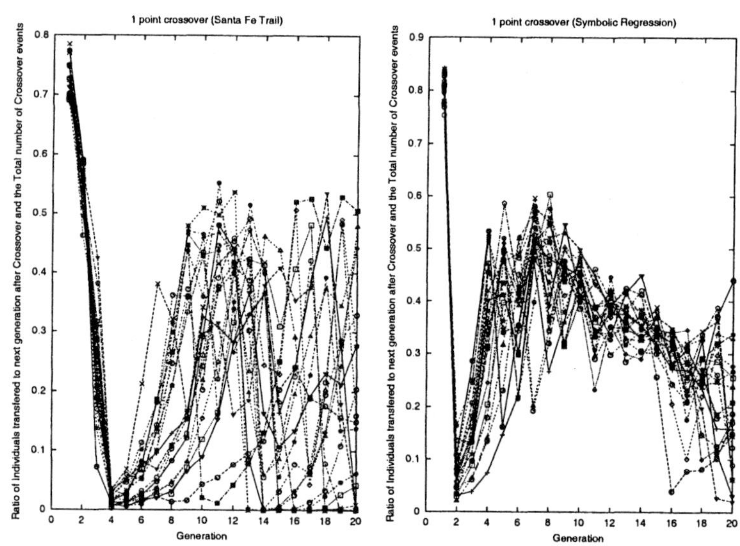

Figure 7.13. Ratio of the number of individuals undergoing one point crossover that have been propagated to the next generation and the total number of crossover events occurring in that generation.

2.3 DISCUSSION

Examining Figures 7.14 and 7.15, we can see the average over 20 runs of the ratio of individuals undergoing crossover that are propagated to the next generation to the total number of crossover events for each generation, and the ratio of the average crossover fragment size to the average chromosome length, respectively. In terms of the ratio of individuals being propagated to the next generation having undergone crossover, we can see that for one point crossover in the case of the Symbolic Regression problem the rate of transfer remains relatively constant throughout the run around the value 0.35. A similar trend can be seen for one point crossover in the case of the Santa Fe trail problem although there is a slight deterioration as runs progress. Looking at the ratio of individuals transfered to the total number of crossover events for individual runs (Figures 7.9, 7.10, 7.11, 7.12 and 7.13), we can see in all cases that in the first few generations this value is extremely high. These results for homologous crossover are not as consistent as those for one point, and, directly compared, appear erratic. They show that the effort required to carry out our version of homologous crossover, and the occasional peak it achieves in terms of individual transfer to each generation, are outweighed by the consistent results produced by the much simpler one point operator.

In general though, we can see the utility of one-point crossover by virtue of the fact that it produces individuals that are capable of being propagated to successive generations, given the steady state replacement strategy.

Looking at the ratio of the average crossover fragment size to the average chromosome length (Figure 7.15), in the case of one-point crossover we get a relatively smooth line around the 0.5 mark for both problems. Similar trends are observed for both types of two-point crossover; however, these are localised to lower values. It can also be seen that the homologous operators are more inconsistent, although on the symbolic regression problem it has a consistently higher value than all other operators. The experimental evidence shows us that crossover results in individuals that are being propagated to the next generation, and that the size ratio of these fragments to the actual genome length is consistent throughout the runs with a value close to 50%. This is in contrast to the results obtained in (Poli and Langdon, 1998) that showed a drop off for all crossover operators except, naturally, for the uniform operator. This is not surprising, however, as they worked exclusively with tree operators. These results showed how the operators examined in this case start off as global search operators but change rapidly to local search operators.

In light of the data obtained, namely the transfer of individuals having undergone crossover to the next generation, it is reasonable to suspect that within GE individuals there exist useful building blocks that are being recombined to produce better performing individuals. With respect to the homologous operator described in (Langdon, 1999) for tree based GP, a lot of effort is required

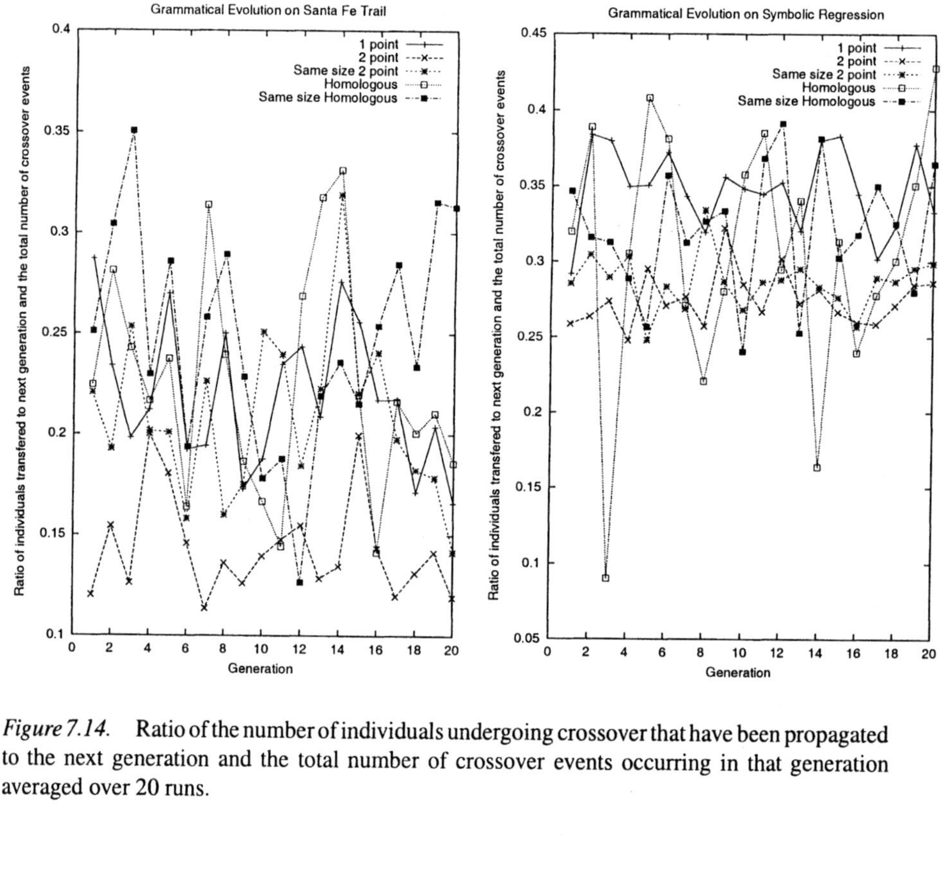

Figure 7.14. Ratio of the number of individuals undergoing crossover that have been propagated to the next generation and the total number of crossover events occurring in that generation averaged over 20 runs.

to carry out this operation, whereas in GE, we get a simple, efficient crossover operator with less effort, that exchanges half the material on average.

3. HEADLESS CHICKEN

We now continue the analysis of crossover in GE by conducting a set of experiments with the objective of testing the hypothesis that crossover is exchanging useful blocks as suggested by the results found in the previous section. To this end we use two main strategies, firstly by turning off crossover, and secondly, by exchanging random blocks in a headless chicken-type crossover (Angeline, 1997). If we observe a decrease in performance in the absence of crossover this would suggest that this operator is providing some useful search, and if the exchange of randomly generated blocks produces an inferior performance to our standard operator this would provide evidence to support the claim that useful building blocks are being exchanged.

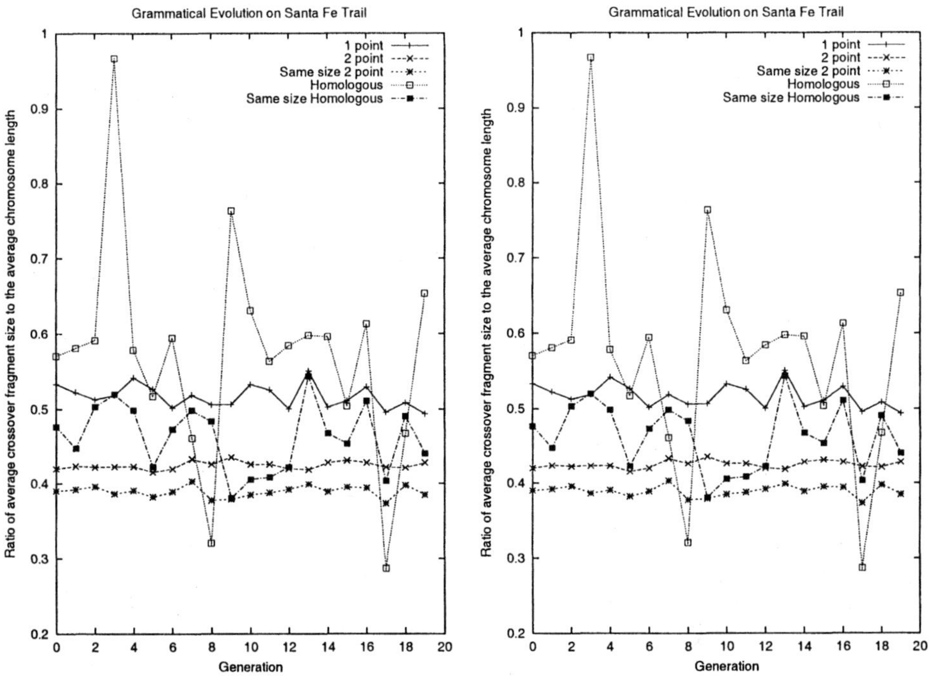

Figure 7.15. Ratio of the average fragment size being swapped and the average chromosome length at each generation averaged over 20 runs.

Two forms of headless chicken crossover were described for trees, with *strong headless chicken crossover* (SHCC) being the most similar to the one adopted here. SHCC operated by creating a random tree for each of the parents selected for crossover, followed by standard sub-tree crossover in GP. The modified parent tree (as opposed to the modified randomly generated tree) being returned. The other form of headless chicken crossover, *weak headless chicken crossover* (WHCC), returned randomly either the modified parent or the modified random tree.

3.1 EXPERIMENTAL APPROACH

The headless chicken operator we adopt selects the fragments to crossover, and replaces them with a randomly generated bit string of the same lengths.

For each experiment 50 runs were carried out on the Santa Fe ant trail and a symbolic regression problem. Performance was ascertained by the cumulative frequency of success.

3.2 RESULTS

Results for the experiments can be seen in Figure 7.16. These graphs clearly demonstrate the damaging effects of the headless chicken crossover, and in the case when crossover is switched off. On the symbolic regression problem GE fails to find solutions in both of these cases, while on the Santa Fe ant trail, the system's success rate falls off dramatically.

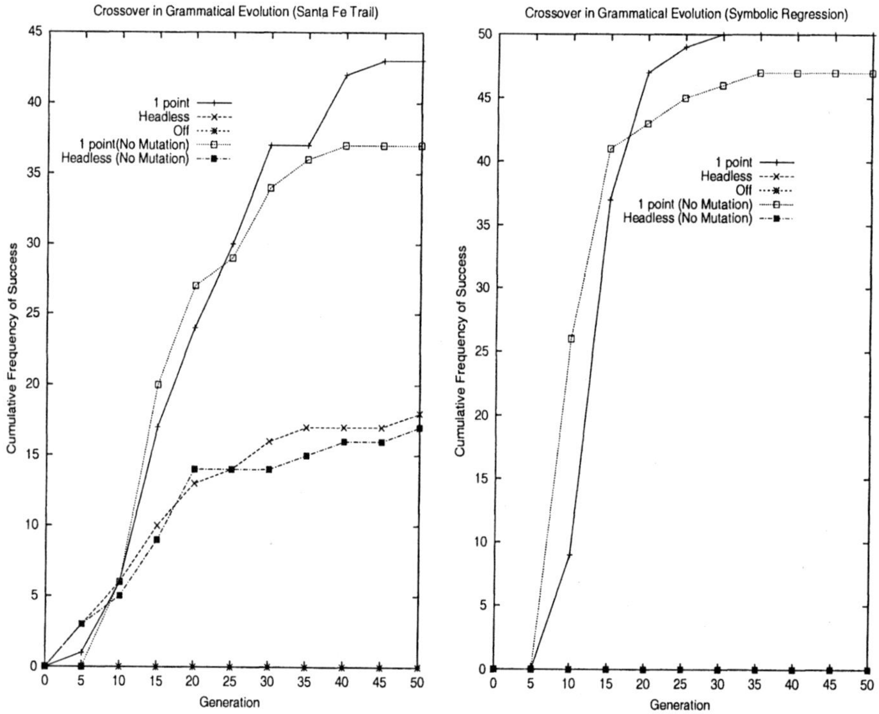

Figure 7.16. A comparison of GE's performance on the Santa Fe ant trail can be seen on the left. The graph clearly demonstrates the damaging effects of the headless chicken crossover, and in the case when crossover is switched off. A comparison of GE's performance on the symbolic regression problem can be seen on the right. When the headless chicken crossover is used the system fails to find solutions, as is also the case when crossover is switched off.

These results clearly demonstrate the power of GE's one point crossover as an operator that successfully exploits an exchange of useful blocks on the problems examined. It also demonstrates that the one point crossover operator is essential to the effective operation of the system.

Experiments were also conducted where the mutation operator was turned off in the cases of both one-point and the homologous crossover operators. The results, see Figure 7.16, demonstrate that, when mutation is turned off in the presence of one-point crossover, there is a decrease in performance when compared to the case where mutation is present. These observations apply to both problem domains examined, and, as such, suggest that mutation plays a beneficial role alongside the successful one-point crossover operator.

3.3 DISCUSSION

The question arises then as to why GE's one point crossover operator is so productive. If we look at the effect the operator plays on a parse tree representation of the programs undergoing crossover, we begin to see more clearly the mechanism of this operator and its search properties.

When mapping a string to an individual, GE always works with the left most non-terminal. Thus, if one were to look at the individual's corresponding parse tree, one would see that the tree is constructed in a pre-order fashion.

Consider the simple grammar :

```
E::=(+ E E) | (- E E) | (* E E) | (% E E) | X | Y
```

which has only a *single* non-terminal. Individuals that legally adhere to this grammar can be represented by GP individuals, as there is only one non-terminal.

As individuals are mapped, their corresponding parse trees are filled in a pre-order fashion. Consider the individual (represented as codon integer values):

```
8 6 4 5 9 4 5 2 0 5 2 2
```

in this case, there is only one rule, with six productions, so we can rewrite the individual with each codon mod six for clarity, and where `x` denotes how much of the individual is expressed :

```
2 0 4 5 3 4 5 x 2 0 5 2 2
```

This individual would produce a parse tree as illustrated in Figure 7.17, which also shows how GP could represent the same individual. The unexpressed codons of the individual are collectively known as the *tail* of the individual. Notice that, at this stage, we are *not* considering individuals that wrap. Only those individuals that completely map in one pass or less are of interest at this stage.

We can now examine crossover using familiar GP concepts, and identify what exactly the difference is between GP and GE crossovers. The first thing to determine is how the simple linear, one point crossover of Grammatical Evolution can be translated into the tree structures of GP.

Crossover in GE selects the first X codons from an individual composed of Z codons, of which Y are expressed. These can be related as :

$$X < Y \leq Z$$

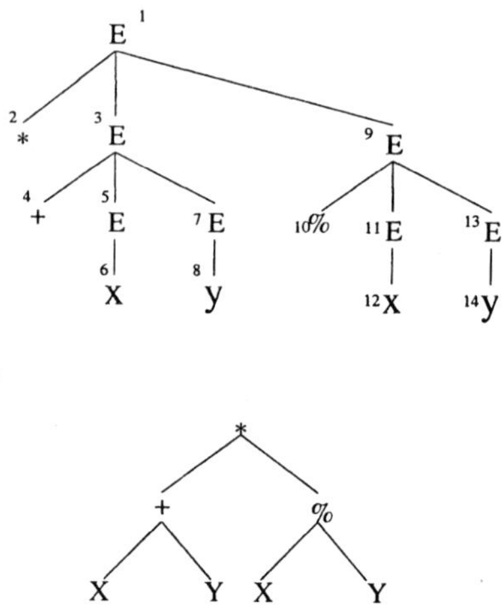

Figure 7.17. (Top) The order in which a parse tree is filled by GE. (Bottom) The corresponding tree as represented by GP.

This means the last $Y - X$ productions are *not* applied to the parse tree. The pre-order nature of the filling of the tree means that a situation like that in Figure 7.18 results. That is, a number of subtrees to the right of the crossover point are removed. We call each of these subtrees *ripple trees* for reasons that will become clear later. The remainder of the tree, to the left of the crossover, is known as the *spine* of the tree, and each of the newly-vacant sites freed by the ripple trees are known as *ripple sites*. Finally, the codons that produced the ripple trees are automatically put back onto the tail in the correct order, so that if they were to be read back again, the same individual would result.

Figure 7.18 also visualises this in terms of GP. When the GE crossover is applied to GP, a similar set of items is created, that is, a spine, ripple sites and ripple trees.

During crossover, this is done to both parents, and they then exchange their tails, as in Figure 7.19. The newly acquired tails are subsequently used to rebuild the parent trees, resulting in two children. This crossover behaviour, which is an inherent property of GE, was first noticed in (Keijzer et al., 2001b) where it was termed *ripple crossover*.

Each of the ripple trees is effectively dismantled and returned to the stack of codons in the individual's tail. Crossover then involves individuals swapping tails so that, when evaluating the offspring, the ripple sites on the spine will be filled using codons from the other parent.

Given the nature of the grammar used in this example, each of the ripple trees from the one parent are used to fill up each of the vacant ripple sites in the corresponding one. If there aren't enough, the remainder of the tail is used to produce more, while if there are too many, the extraneous ones are left on the

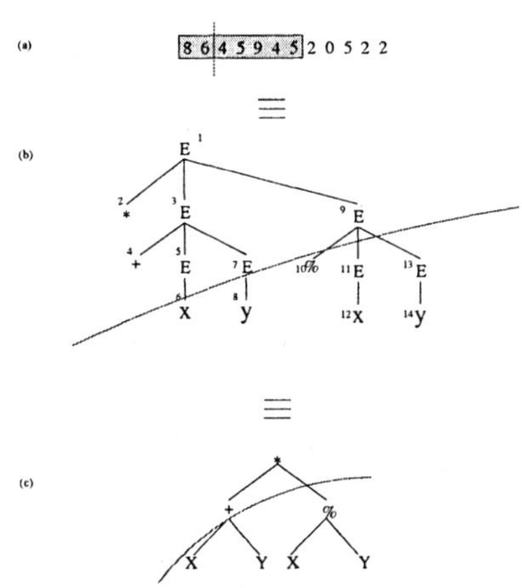

Figure 7.18. The ripple effect of one-point crossover illustrated using an example GE individual represented as a string of codon integer values (a) and its equivalent derivation (b) and parse trees (c). The codon integer values in (a) will be used to generate the rule number to be selected from the grammar outlined, with the part shaded gray corresponding to the values used to produce the trees in (b) and (c). Figure 7.19 shows the resulting spine with ripple sites and tails.

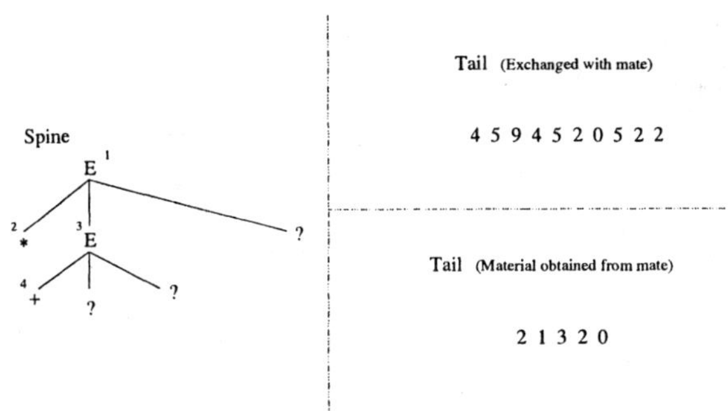

Figure 7.19. An individual during crossover. Its newly formed tail is about to be swapped with the other parent's tail.

tail. This happens because there is only one non-terminal, which is the same as in GP, that is, the grammar is a *closed grammar*, which adheres to the closure principle that any non-terminal and take any other non-terminal or terminal as an argument.

However, in standard GE, the closure principle doesn't hold, and there is no guarantee that the tail from the other parent will be of the same length, or even that it is used in a similar place on the other spine. This means that a codon that represented which choice to make could suddenly be expected to make a choice from a completely different non-terminal, possibly with a different number of choices. Fortunately, GE evaluates codons *in context*, that is, the exact meaning of a codon is determined by those codons that immediately precede it. Thus, we can say that GE codons have *intrinsic polymorphism*, as they can be used in any part of the grammar; furthermore, if the meaning of one codon changes, the change cascades, or "ripples" through all the rest of the codons. This means that a group of codons that coded a particular sub-tree on one spine can code an entirely different sub-tree when employed by another spine. The power of intrinsic polymorphism can even reach between the ripple trees, in that if one no longer needs all its codons, they are passed to the next ripple tree and, conversely, if it requires more codons, it can obtain them from its neighbouring ripple tree.

4. CONCLUSIONS

We began this chapter with an investigation into a new homologous crossover operator designed for GE, to discover that it was no better than the standard one-point crossover originally adopted.

Further analysis, using a headless chicken-type operator, and by switching off crossover altogether, revealed the power this one-point operator brought to GE.

In the writing of this chapter, the value of linear chromosomes in general, and the GE system in particular, became quite clear to us. Ripple crossover occurs effectively for free in a linear system, because of the pre-order nature of tree construction, and results in, on average, 50% of the material being exchanged during a crossover event. Furthermore, the phenomenon of *intrinsic polymorphism* demonstrates the utility of context sensitive genes (groups of codons), that is, genes that can change their behaviour depending on the manner in which they are used. Rather elegantly, although the genes are polymorphic, they will always return to their initial state if used in the same manner again.

Chapter 8

EXTENSIONS & APPLICATIONS

We said in chapter 1 that the beauty of grammars is that they provide a single mechanism that can be used to describe all manner of complex structures. Not only can all sorts of different problems can be tackled simply by changing the grammar, so too can different *algorithms* be emulated just by using the appropriate grammar. This chapter gives an overview of current work in extending GE being carried out at various institutions, and demonstrates that GE is more of a family of algorithms, rather than a single method.

Given the rich modularity of the system, there is much scope to enhance its various components. These enhancements can range from a simple change in the grammar used by the system, which as we will see can have radical changes on behaviour (e.g., a grammar that transforms GE into a position independent genetic algorithm), to the use of a search algorithm based on alternative paradigms to evolutionary computation, to more subtle changes in the complexity of mapping functions used in place of the standard modulo operator.

1. TRANSLATION

We present an alternative translation function, called the Bucket Rule, for Grammatical Evolution that has shown promise in recent experiments on bitstring generation problems.

Consider a simple context-free grammar that can be used to generate variable length bitstrings:

```
<bitstring>::= <bit> | <bit> <bitstring>.

<bit>  ::= 0 | 1.
```

This context-free grammar has two non-terminal symbols, each of which have two production rules. In GE a string of codons are maintained, each consisting of typically 8 bits of information. The modulo rule defines a degenerate mapping from those 8 bits of information to a choice for a production rule in the following way. Given a set of n non-terminals with a corresponding number of production rules $[c_1, \ldots, c_n]$ and given the current symbol r, the mapping rule used is:

$$choice(r) = codon\%c_r \tag{8.1}$$

This modulo rule ensures that the codon value is mapped into the interval $[0, c_r]$ and thus represents a valid choice for a production rule. As the codons themselves are drawn from the interval $[0, 255]$ in the case of 8-bit codons, the mapping rule is degenerate: many codon values map to the same choice of rules. Unfortunately, in the case of the context-free grammar given above, the modulo rule will map all even codon values to the first rule and all odd values to the second rule, regardless of the non-terminal symbol that is active. In effect, when using this context-free grammar in combination with the modulo mapping rule, it is the least significant bit in the codon value that fully determines the mapping, that is, all other 7 bits are redundant.

In the context of the untyped crossover and associated intrinsic polymorphism that is usually used in GE (Keijzer et al., 2001b) — strings of codon values taken from two independently drawn points from the genotypes can be swapped. Here it is possible that a codon value that was used to encode for the `<bitstring>` non-terminal can be used to encode a choice for the `<bit>` non-terminal, due to intrinsic polymorphism, that is a codon can specify a rule for every non-terminal in the grammar and therefore, has meaning in every context.

Codon Value	**non-terminal Symbol**	
	`<bit>`	`<bitstring>`
0	0	`<bit>`
1	1	`<bit> <bitstring>`

A codon value of 0, for example, always selects the first production rule for every non-terminal (i.e., in above, `<bit>` would become 0, and `<bitstring>` would become `<bit>`). Thus regardless of the context (the non-terminal) in which the codon is used, it will have a fixed choice of production rules. It would be better for GE's intrinsic polymorphism if this linkage did not exist, thus each non-terminal's production rule choice is independent of all the other non-terminals when intrinsic polymorphism comes into play.

The linkage between production rules belonging to different non-terminal symbols, in combination with untyped variation operators introduces a bias in the search process. This bias is undesirable because it depends on the layout of the program and its impact on the search is not clear. In effect this means that the order in which the rules are defined are expected to make a difference to the search efficiency.

To remove this bias the mapping rule can be changed. Given again our set of productions for n non-terminal symbols $[c_1, \ldots, c_n]$, the codon values are now taken from the interval $[0, \prod_{i=1}^{n} c_i]$. The mapping rule is subsequently changed to:

$$choice(r) = \frac{codon}{\prod_{i=1}^{r-1} c_i} \% c_r \tag{8.2}$$

This rule is simply the standard method for mapping multi-dimensional matrices into a contiguous array of values. With this rule, every legal codon value encodes a unique set of production rules, one from each non-terminal. In the grammar discussed here, the codons are drawn from $[0, 3]$. The codon values encode for the production rules given the non-terminals in the following way:

Codon Value	**non-terminal Symbol**	
	`<bit>`	`<bitstring>`
0	0	`<bit>`
1	1	`<bit> <bitstring>`
2	0	`<bit> <bitstring>`
3	1	`<bit>`

We choose the name *buckets* because we believe the manner in which a single codon value can code for a number of different choices across different rules is similar to the manner in which keys can hash to identical locations in certain hashing algorithms.

2. ALTERNATIVE SEARCH STRATEGIES

All the experiments presented in this book use a Genetic Algorithm to produce the binary strings. However, given the separation of search and solution space provided by GE, any iterative search algorithm that is capable of producing binary strings can be employed.

Recent work (O'Sullivan, 2003) (O'Sullivan and Ryan, 2002) has compared the use of a number of approaches, including random search, simulated annealing, hill climbing, Evolutionary Programming, Evolutionary Strategies and Genetic Algorithms. In general, the population based methods performed best, and, of those, a Genetic Algorithm performed the best.

The key differences between the GA used and the other population based methods were the use of variable length genomes and the size of the population used, although all comparisons were made using an identical number of evaluations.

Although the GA was clearly the best performer on the set of benchmarks used, this research is at too early a stage to make any definitive recommendations about using a GA exclusively. One curious result was that EP and ES performed very similarly, even though there are a number of fundamental differences between the two methods, not least of which is the fact that EP doesn't employ crossover.

3. GRAMMAR DEFINED INTRONS

The benefit, or otherwise, of introns in evolutionary computation have been hotly debated for some time (e.g., see (Levenick, 1991; Levenick, 1999; Altenberg, 1994; Angeline, 1994; Nordin and Banzhaf, 1995a; Nordin et al., 1996; Wu and Lindsay, 1995; Andre and Teller, 1996; Wineberg and Oppacher, 1996; Haynes, 1996; Wu and Lindsay, 1996; Lobo et al., 1998; Smith and Harries, 1998)). In the standard implementation of GE, introns can only occur at the end of a chromosome due to the nature of the mapping process. The role of an intron in the preservation of building blocks due to destructive crossover events is therefore minimised in GE.

Some preliminary investigations of a mechanism by which they may be incorporated into GE through the grammar, and the effects introns might have on the performance of GE have been conducted (O'Neill et al., 2001c). The mechanism by which introns have been incorporated is called Grammar Defined Introns, whereby the grammar is used to incorporate introns into the genome. This is achieved by allowing codons to be skipped over during the mapping process, by using `introns` as a choice(s) for non-terminals.

For example, the following non-terminal uses an intron as a rule:

```
<bit> :: =  0
         |  1
         |  intron
```

When a codon evaluates to the `intron` rule being selected we simply skip over this codon, and the code undergoing the mapping is unchanged. In this case the non-terminal `<bit>` would remain as `<bit>` if the `intron` rule is selected, and the next codon is read.

Alternatively, and more simply, a similar effect is achieved by using the non-terminal symbol in place of the reserved non-terminal intron. For example the same grammar above could be rewritten as:

```
<bit> :: =  0
         |  1
         |  <bit>
```

In this case the codon value can be used to select the production, where `<bit>` is replaced with itself, thus having the same effect as the special intron symbol without the extra overhead of handling this case.

Further experimentation and analysis are required on grammar defined introns before any definitive claims as to their effects, either positive or negative, can be made.

4. GAUGE

GAUGE (*Genetic Algorithms using Grammatical Evolution*) is a Genetic Algorithm that attempts to overcome the position dependence issue by extending GE with an attribute grammar that makes the system behave like a position-independent Genetic Algorithm. The system is far less susceptible to the disruption often associated with crossover, as the system can automatically move important genes closer together as a run progresses.

The common view of Genetic Programming is that, given a particular problem statement, a program that satisfies the fitness function is to be generated. In other words, *given a set of terminals, how should they be arranged so that the fitness function is satisfied?*

The approach GAUGE takes is that *all* problems, even those traditionally considered the topic of Genetic Algorithms, can be looked upon as automatic programming ones. In particular, if one considers a problem to have two parts, that is, not only *what values should the genes have?* but also *where should the genes reside?*, it is reasonable to compare this class of problem with those above.

When applying GAUGE to a Genetic Algorithm problem, one uses a set of codon pairs, one for each gene position in the original problem. An individual is processed in a similar manner to GE, by moding each gene by an appropriate value to produce a useful value. Like GE, the codons are 8-bit values, also giving a degenerate encoding. For GAUGE, the values required are the position that the pair will code for, and the value for that bit position. To produce these values, a list of *unspecified* positions is maintained, that is, those positions that have not been given a value yet. Thus, even when evolving individuals that are binary strings, GAUGE always has a distinct genotype and phenotype.

A simple way to represent the binary strings positions and values in a grammar is as follows:

$$
\begin{array}{ll}
<S>_n ::= & \epsilon \\
 & \text{Cond}: <S>_n = 0; \\
 & \mid <P>_n <V>_a <S>_n \\
 & <P>_n := <S>_n ; <S>_n := <S>_n - 1; \\
 & \text{Cond}: <S>_n > 0 \\
<V>_a ::= & 0 \\
 & \mid 1 \\
 & \mid : \\
 & \mid \text{a-1} \\
<P>_n ::= & 0 \\
 & \mid 1 \\
 & \mid : \\
 & \mid \text{n-1}
\end{array}
$$

The mapping happens in two stages; first a set of (position, value) pairs are generated using the above grammar, while the second step simply puts them in the correct order. The number of bits in the phenotype is given by the attribute n, so that a string of n bits is generated due to the productions corresponding to the non-terminal $<S>_n$. The first rule for $<S>_n$ terminates the string if the value of n is zero, as on the addition of a new bit to the growing string the value of n is decremented, which is specified by the second production for this rule. The productions <V> and <P> are straightforward in this case as the values (specified by <V>) are integers from zero to $a - 1$, where a is the alphabet size of phenotype string (e.g., for a binary string a=2) and an attribute of <V>. The positions, given by <P>, are simply integers from zero to $n - 1$.

A more elegant way to represent these position and value pairs is given in the following grammar. In this case, the ordered binary string is constructed directly by the attribute grammar itself.

A phenotype string's length is generated in a similar manner to the previous grammar, as given by the non-terminal <S>, in terms of it's use of the attribute n (i.e., length of phenotypic string to be generated). The difference lies in the manner in which the positions are specified, and their placement into the final phenotype position.

In this case, there are a number of attributes associated with the developing string, of particular importance is the $array$ attribute, which maintains an array of free locations (positions that are as yet unspecified) in the phenotype string. When a new <P> is specified from the non-terminal <S> a desired location is given by the next codon. The desired location is copied to the non-terminal $<F>_{val}$ using the attribute, val, where it is used to determine what the final phenotypic location will actually be. To achieve this some management attributes are required, namely, v and c. v counts through the number of vacant positions encountered, and c counts the total number of positions encountered (both vacant and occupied). The three rules in <F> determine the following respectively:

1 Is this the correct location AND is it vacant? If so, return the value of c, create a <V> production for the value and give a recursive call to <S> for the next pair (i.e., position and value).

2 This is not the correct location, but it is vacant. Increment the counter into the array AND the count of vacants.

3 This is not vacant - note that this is the ONLY check that has to be made, we don't care if it is the desired location or not. Increment the counter into the array only.

By simply generating a non-terminal <F> in the developing string the rules of this production call themselves recursively until the specified phenotypic position is determined in the $array$ attribute. When this occurs the non-terminal <V> is invoked, finally allowing the specification of the value to be placed at this previously determined position. The mapping process finishes with the output of the final phenotypic binary string.

$<S>_{n.array}$ ::= ϵ
Cond : $<S>_n=0$;
| $<P>_{n.array}$
Cond : $<S>_n>0$;

$<V>_n$ ::= 0
| 1
| :
| n-1

$<P>_{n.array}$ ::= $<F>_{c.array.val.n.v}$
$<F>_v:=0$;
$<F>_c:=0$;
$<F>_{array}:= <P>_{array}$;
$<F>_n:= <P>_n$;
$<F>_{val}:=0$;
| $<F>_{c.array.val.n.v}$
$<F>_v:=0$;
$<F>_c:=0$;
$<F>_{array}:= <P>_{array}$;
$<F>_n:= <P>_n$;
$<F>_{val}:=1$;
:
| $<F>_{c.array.val.n.v}$
$<F>_v:=0$;
$<F>_c:=0$;
$<F>_{array}:= <P>_{array}$;
$<F>_n:= <P>_n$;
$<F>_{val}:=n-1$;

$<F>_{c.array.val.n.v}$::= $<F>_c <V><S>_{n.array}$
$<S>_n = <F>_n-1$;
$<S>_{array} = <F>_{array}$
$<S>_{array} = <S>_{array[<F>_c]}$
Cond : $(<F>_c>=<F>_v)\&\&(<F>_{array[<F>_c]}= -1)$
| $<F>_{c.array.val.n.v}$
$<F>_c:=<F>_c+1;<F>_v:=<F>_c+1$;
Cond : $<F>_{array[<F>_c]}= -1$
| $<F>_{c.array.val.n.v}$
$<F>_c:=<F>_c+1$;
Cond : $<F>_{array[<F>_c]}! = -1$

4.1 PROBLEMS

This section introduces two problems to which standard GAs, GAUGE and messyGA have been applied (Ryan et al., 2002b). To show that GAUGE is a capable system, we used the standard onemax problem; to illustrate its position-independent nature, we have devised a deceptive ordering problem, based on the Mastermind[1] game.

4.1.1 ONEMAX

We ran the standard onemax problem (i.e., where the fitness of an individual is the sum of the bits which are equal to 1) using lengths of 50, 100 and 150 bits per individual. To choose which GA to compare GAUGE to, we measured the performance of several systems, shown in Table 8.1.

We included GAs using 8 bits per gene in this comparison, as they use the same degenerate encoding as GAUGE, running these systems up to 25000 evaluations, using population sizes of 50, 100, 200, 400, 800 and 1600 individuals. It was found that the generational algorithms could not solve the problem with these parameters, but steady-state algorithms performed well (with no significant difference between 1 or 8 bits per codon). We therefore compared GAUGE to a simple GA with steady-state, using 1 bit per codon (setting SGAss).

We have also compared GAUGE with messyGA (Goldberg et al., 1991a) (using the code available from the IlliGAL server (IlliGAL, 2003), explained in (Deb and Goldberg, 1991)), and tried several combinations of settings for it (see Table 8.2), choosing the one that best performed on this given problem (setting STD). We wanted to test all systems with string lengths of up to 400 bits, but ran into difficulties, since some of the messyGA runs (for length 150) demanded over 1.1GB of memory (i.e., over one thousand times more than GAUGE or the simple GA) to execute, due to messyGA's variable length individuals and variable population sizes; this made running the experiments a very long task, and using longer strings was physically impossible[2].

Table 8.1. General settings used in all GAs and GAUGE.

Parameters	*SGA*	*SGAss*	*GA*	*GAss*	*GAUGE*
Replacement strategy	gener.	s-state	gener.	s-state	s-state
Selection routine	r-wheel	r-wheel	r-wheel	r-wheel	r-wheel
Bits per gene	1	1	8	8	8+8
Number of runs	100	100	100	100	100
Probability of crossover	0.9	0.9	0.9	0.9	0.9
Probability of mutation	0.01	0.01	0.01	0.01	0.01

[1]Mastermind is a registered trademark of Pressman Toy Corporation, by agreement with Invicta Toys and Games, Ltd., UK.

[2]These experiments were run on a dual-processor Pentium III 1GHz computer, with 2GB of shared memory available.

Table 8.2. Tested combinations of settings for messyGA algorithm (Deb and Goldberg, 1991; Goldberg et al., 1991b).

Parameters	*STD*	*OPT1*	*OPT2*	*OPT3*
Maximum era	3	3	3	3
Probability of cut	0.02	0.02	0.02	0.02
Probability of splice	1.0	1.0	1.0	1.0
Probability of allelic mut.	0.00	0.01	0.01	0.01
Probability of genic mut.	0.00	0.01	0.01	0.01
Thresholding	0	0	0	1
Tiebreaking	0	0	0	1
Reduced initial pop.	1	0	0	0
Extra pop. members	0	0	0	0
Copies	10, 1, 1	1, 1, 1	10, 1, 1	10, 1, 1
Total generations	100, 100, 100	100, 100, 100	100, 100, 100	100, 100, 100
Juxtapositional popsize	100, 100, 100	100, 100, 100	100, 100, 100	100, 100, 100

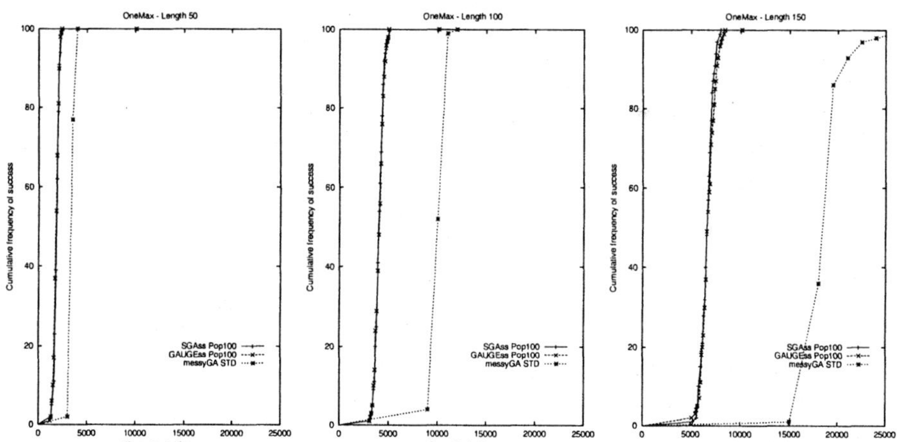

Figure 8.1. Results for onemax problem.

4.1.2 RESULTS

We can see in Figure 8.1 that GAUGE has a similar behaviour to the simple GA, across all individual lengths (this behaviour was also visible across all population sizes). This shows that GAUGE does not suffer a performance loss from its genotype to phenotype mapping. We can also see that the messyGA with the STD settings has a lower performance than both the simple GA and GAUGE, and its performance gets worse relative to those two systems with longer strings.

4.2 MASTERMIND - A DECEPTIVE ORDERING VERSION

In the original Mastermind game, one player is the *codebreaker* and tries to deduce a hidden configuration of four coloured pins, set by the *codemaker*, by having a maximum of ten guesses at it. The pins come in six different colours. Each guess has a score of black and white markers, a black marker indicating that one of the pins has the right colour and is in the right position, and a white marker indicating that a pin has the right colour, but is badly placed. More information can be found online at (Nelson, 1999). There have been some attemps at applying genetic algorithms to solve this game (Bernier and Herraiz, 1996).

Some deceptive ordering problems have been defined in earlier work (check (Kargupta et al., 1992) and (Knjazew and Goldberg, 2000) for examples), and with similarities to Mastermind. We wanted, however, a problem with the following characteristics:

- easy to implement and quick to evaluate;
- easy to scale difficulty;
- defined search space with local optima;
- illustrates the ordering performance of algorithms.

Our version of Mastermind is therefore slightly different. First of all, we work with numbers to represent colours, and the information available to the *codebreaker* is somewhat reduced. When a combination of pins is to be evaluated, it receives one point for each pin that has the right colour, and if all pins are in the correct order then an additional fitness point is attributed - in other words, information about the correct placement of pins is only given if the whole string is correct. Some examples are shown in Table 8.3.

There is a deceptive aspect to this problem. If an individual is composed of all the correct pins but in the wrong order, it has reached a local optimum; since at least two pins are wrongly placed, then the global optimum is always at least at a hamming distance of two from every local optimum (since at least two values will need to be changed).

There is a good degree of control over the size and shape of the search space. By recalling combinatorial notions, we see that the size of the search space (i.e. all possible combinations of p pins using c colours) is given by c^p.

We can also calculate the number of local optima by using the formula:

$$\frac{p!}{\prod_{i=0}^{n}(x_i)!}$$

Table 8.3. Examples of evaluation of individuals using the Mastermind fitness function.

Solution: 3 2 1 3	
Individual	Fitness
0 2 1 0	2 points
0 1 2 0	2 points
2 1 2 0	2 points
3 1 2 0	3 points
3 1 2 3	4 points
3 2 1 3	5 points

where
n = number of colours in solution
x_i = number of times colour i appears in solution

4.2.1 RESULTS

We start by comparing GAUGE to an ordinary GA. To avoid redundant encoding in the simple GA, we used only cases of four and eight colours (encoded by two and three bits per codon, respectively). All the different GA settings (as described in Table 8.1) were again tested, but using the mentioned bits per codon to encode colours with the simple GA. We then used combinations with four, six, eight and ten pins for each number of colours. The solutions used for each combination are shown in Table 8.4, and were created using random strings of numbers from 0 to c, from which the first p elements were extracted.

Our results showed GAs with generational replacement behaved better with small population sizes, whereas steady-state GAs worked better with larger ones. We also tested the statistical significance of the performance of GAUGE and the GAs using steady-state, on the average fitness and best fitness across all runs using a student t-test, and a bootstrap test for confirmation.

The results showed GAUGE outperforming all GA flavours across all the experiments, with a statistically significant difference on the majority of the experiments; Table 8.5 shows the percentage of successful runs, after 25000 evaluations, for SGAss and GAUGE, with all population sizes, on the tested combinations of colours and pins. Example results for 4 colours, 8 pins, are shown in Figure 8.2, with population sizes 100 and 800. These graphs plot the number of fitness function calls versus the cumulative frequency of success of 100 different runs.

We then moved onto comparing the messyGA with GAUGE, and GAUGE again outperformed the messyGA across all its settings (as shown in Table 8.2).

However, since the messyGA encodes positions for bits, whereas GAUGE encodes positions for values (which can directly represent colours), this gives GAUGE an advantage. We therefore devised a new version of GAUGE (which we shall refer to as GAUGE1BIT) to encode positions for bits, rather than for full values, and compared both systems.

Table 8.4. Solutions used across all systems for each colours/pins combination.

#Colours/Pins	*Solution*
4 Colours, 4 pins	3 2 1 3
4 Colours, 6 pins	3 2 1 3 1 3
4 Colours, 8 pins	3 2 1 3 1 3 2 0
4 Colours, 10 pins	3 2 1 3 1 3 2 0 1 1
8 Colours, 4 pins	7 6 1 3
8 Colours, 6 pins	7 6 1 3 1 7
8 Colours, 8 pins	7 6 1 3 1 7 2 4
8 Colours, 10 pins	7 6 1 3 1 7 2 4 1 5

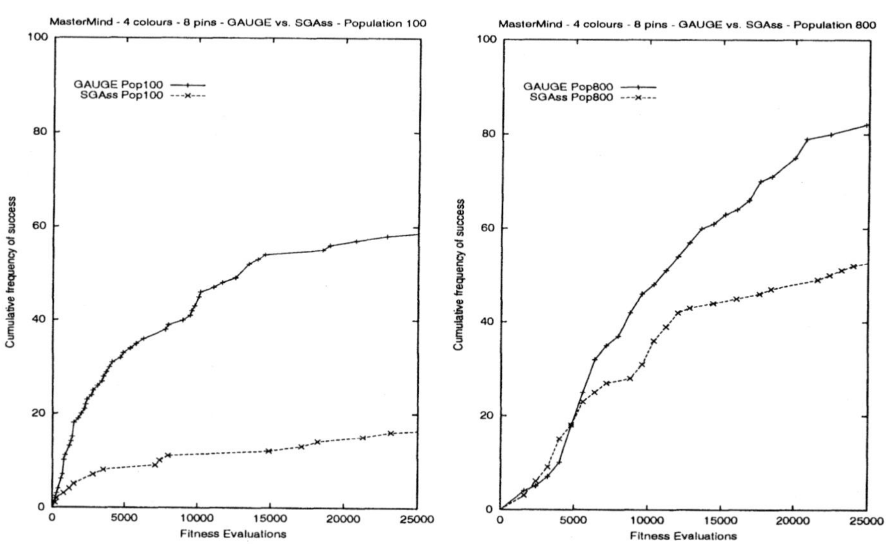

Figure 8.2. Simple GA vs. GAUGE, MASTERMIND with 4 colours, 8 pins.

GAUGE1BIT showed a better performance than all the messyGA settings, as can be seen in Figure 8.3, which shows the cumulative frequency of success of 100 runs plotted against the number of function calls. Table 8.6 shows the percentage of successful runs after 25000 evaluations, for all combinations of colours and pins tested. We noticed that allelic and genic mutation seemed to

Table 8.5. Percentage of successful runs after 25000 evaluations, for SGAss and GAUGE, for all tested combinations of colours/pins, across all population sizes.

		SGAss					
Population size:		*50*	*100*	*200*	*400*	*800*	*1600*
4colours	4 pins	96%	100%	100%	100%	100%	100%
4colours	6 pins	59%	87%	99%	100%	100%	100%
4colours	8 pins	11%	16%	26%	32%	52%	63%
4colours	10 pins	0%	2%	2%	9%	11%	6%
8colours	4 pins	43%	64%	83%	97%	99%	100%
8colours	6 pins	8%	18%	44%	74%	86%	96%
8colours	8 pins	0%	2%	0%	2%	2%	6%
8colours	10 pins	0%	0%	0%	0%	0%	0%
		GAUGE					
Population size:		*50*	*100*	*200*	*400*	*800*	*1600*
4colours	4 pins	100%	100%	100%	100%	100%	100%
4colours	6 pins	100%	100%	100%	100%	100%	100%
4colours	8 pins	45%	58%	81%	83%	82%	79%
4colours	10 pins	14%	20%	20%	21%	24%	17%
8colours	4 pins	95%	100%	100%	100%	100%	100%
8colours	6 pins	74%	94%	99%	100%	100%	100%
8colours	8 pins	7%	15%	16%	14%	10%	6%
8colours	10 pins	1%	1%	0%	1%	0%	0%

increase the performance of the messyGA, and setting OPT3, with thresholding and tiebreaking enabled, had a slightly better performance than all other messyGA settings.

Table 8.6. Percentage of successful runs after 25000 evaluations, comparing all tested settings of messyGA with GAUGE1BIT, for all combinations of colours/pins.

		messyGA				*GAUGE1BIT*	
	Setting:	*STD*	*OPT1*	*OPT2*	*OPT3*	*Pop100*	*Pop800*
4colours	4 pins	73%	72%	94%	97%	100%	100%
4colours	6 pins	41%	41%	81%	96%	100%	100%
4colours	8 pins	3%	5%	19%	21%	45%	55%
4colours	10 pins	1%	1%	7%	4%	6%	6%
8colours	4 pins	27%	27%	50%	84%	88%	100%
8colours	6 pins	6%	8%	21%	22%	22%	56%
8colours	8 pins	1%	0%	0%	0%	0%	0%
8colours	10 pins	0%	0%	0%	0%	0%	0%

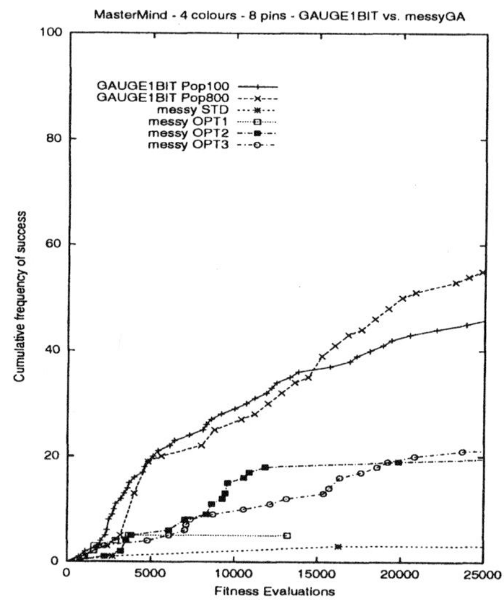

Figure 8.3. GAUGE1BIT vs. messyGA, MASTERMIND with 4 colours, 8 pins.

4.3 DISCUSSION

The results reported for the onemax problem show that GAUGE is a system that works. It performs no worse than a simple GA for that problem, showing that it doesn't suffer a performance loss from its genotype to phenotype mapping, or from its position-independence implementation. Moreover, no significant computational effort is required, due to the use of a simple attribute grammar.

Regarding the Mastermind results, they show an encouraging performance from GAUGE. Either encoding the position of values (directly transformed in colours) or encoding bits (later combined to form colours), GAUGE outperformed all other systems analysed, across a range of increasingly difficult combinations of colours and pins, thus managing to escape the deception of local optima. Moreover, this was achieved without any parameter tuning, and the results were only limited by the number of fitness function calls. It would be interesting to increase that number, and see how far GAUGE can go.

4.4 CONCLUSIONS AND FUTURE WORK

One of the known downfalls of genetic algorithms is the lack of position specification, which leads to convergence to local optima on ordering problems. By applying the principles behind Grammatical Evolution, GAUGE can co-evolve the representation with the solution. With its genotype/phenotype distinction, position/value separation, and small overhead processing required,

GAUGE was successful on both a typical GA benchmark, onemax, and a new deceptive problem introduced in this paper, Mastermind.

Further work will involve testing GAUGE on other problems, from harder versions of Mastermind (to test scalability) to linkage problems, and comparing GAUGE to other more recent and complex competent genetic algorithms.

5. CHORUS

Chorus is another position independent system, although, unlike GAUGE, it is used for evolving programs (Ryan et al., 2002a; Azad et al., 2002). This scheme is coarsely based on the manner in nature in which genes produce proteins that regulate the metabolic pathways of the cell. The phenotype is the behaviour of the cells metabolism, which corresponds to the development of the computer program in our case. In this procedure, the actual protein encoded by a gene is the same regardless of the position of the gene within the genome. In a similar manner to GE, Chorus uses a chromosome of eight bit numbers (termed codons) to dictate which rules from the grammar to apply. However, unlike the intrinsically polymorphic codons of GE, each codon in Chorus corresponds to a particular production rule, similar to the GADS system, although Chorus doesn't have quite the same issue with introns as GADS did.

```
<expr> ::= <expr> <op> <expr>      (0)
         | ( <expr> <op> <expr> ) (1)
         | <pre-op> ( <expr> )    (2)
         | <var>                  (3)
<op> ::= + (4) | - (5) | / (6) | * (7)
<pre-op> ::= Sin (8) | Cos (9) | Exp (A) | Log (B)
<var> ::= 1.0 (C) | X (D)
```

For example, consider the following individual that will use the above grammar:

28	21	42	27	27	17	31	18	15	45	55	21	31	27	65

which can be looked upon as a collection of hard coded production rules. A rule is obtained from a codon by simply moding it by the *total* number of production rules. In this case, that is 14, giving us, in hex:

0	7	0	D	D	3	3	4	1	3	D	7	3	D	9

Each codon encodes a *protein* which, in our case is a production rule. Proteins in this case are enzymes that regulate the metabolism of the cell. These proteins can combine with other proteins (production rules in our case) to take particular *metabolic pathways*, which are, essentially, phenotypes. The more of a codon that is present in the genome, the greater the *concentration* of the corresponding protein will be during the mapping process (Lewin, 1999). In a coarse model of this, we introduce the notion of a *concentration table.* The concentration table is simply a measure of the concentrations of each of the proteins at any given time, and is initialised with each concentration at zero. At any stage, the protein with the greatest concentration will be chosen, switching on the corresponding metabolic pathway, thus, the switching on of a metabolic pathway corresponds to the development of the forming solution with the application of a production rule.

During the mapping process, a number of decisions have to be made, for example, the start symbol `<expr>` has four possible mappings. When such a decision has to be resolved, the relevant area of the concentration table is consulted. In this case, the entries for the first four rules are examined.

Decision resolution in this case is analogous to a group of voices, vying for attention where the loudest voice, i.e., the protein with the greatest concentration level, will come out on top. However if there is not a clear winner, then the genome is read until one of the relevant proteins becomes dominant.

While searching for a particular concentration, it is probable that some other proteins, unrelated to the current choice, will be encountered. In this case, their corresponding concentration is increased, so when that production rule is involved in a choice, it will be more likely to win. This is where the position independence aspect of the system comes in to play; the crucial thing is the presence or otherwise of a codon, while its position is less so. Importantly, *absolute* position almost never matters, while occasionally, *relative* position (to another codon) is important.

Once the choice has been made, the concentration of the chosen production rule is decremented. However, it is not possible for a concentration to fall below zero.

Chorus always works with the left most non-terminal in the current sentence, and continues until either there are none left, or it encounters a choice for which there are no codons to promote the concentrations. In the latter case, the individual responsible is given a suitably chastening fitness measure to ensure that it is unlikely to engage in any kind of reproductive activity in the subsequent generation.

5.1 EXAMPLE INDIVIDUAL

Using the grammar and individual from the previous section we will now demonstrate the genotype-phenotype mapping of a Chorus individual.
For clarity, we also show the normalised values of each codon, that is, the codons mod 14. This is only done for readability, as in the Chorus system, the genome is only read on demand and not decoded until needed.

0	7	0	D	D	3	3	4	1	3	D	7	3	D	9

The first step in decoding the individual is the creation of the concentration table. There is one entry for each production rule (0..D), each of which is initially empty. The table is split across two lines to aid readability.

Rule #	0	1	2	3	4	5	6
Concentration							
Rule #	7	8	9	A	B	C	D
Concentration							

The sentence starts as `<expr>`, so the first choice must be made from productions 0..3, that is:

```
<expr>     ::=  <expr> <op> <expr>    (0)
              | ( <expr> <op> <expr>) (1)
              | <pre-op> ( <expr> )   (2)
              | <var>                 (3)
```

None of these have a non zero concentration yet, so we must read the first codon from the genome, which will cause it to produce its protein. This codon decodes to 0, which is involved in the current choice. Its concentration is amended, and the choice made. As this is the only production in the current choice that has any concentration, it will be selected, and the current expression becomes:

```
<expr><op><expr>
```

The process is repeated for the next leftmost non-terminal, which is another `expr`. In this case, again the concentrations are at their minimal level for the possible choices, so another codon is read and processed. This codon is 7, which is not involved in the current choice, so we move on and keep reading the genome till we find rule 0 which is a relevant rule. Meanwhile we increment the concentration of rule 7. Similar to the previous step, production rule #0 is chosen, so the expression is now

```
<expr><op><expr><op><expr>
```

Next attempt to find a rule for the non-terminal `expr`, produces rule 3, incrementing the concentration for rule *D* twice in the process. The expression now becomes

```
<var><op><expr><op><expr>
```

The current state of the concentration table is

Rule #	0	1	2	3	4	5	6
Concentration							
Rule #	7	8	9	A	B	C	D
Concentration	1						2

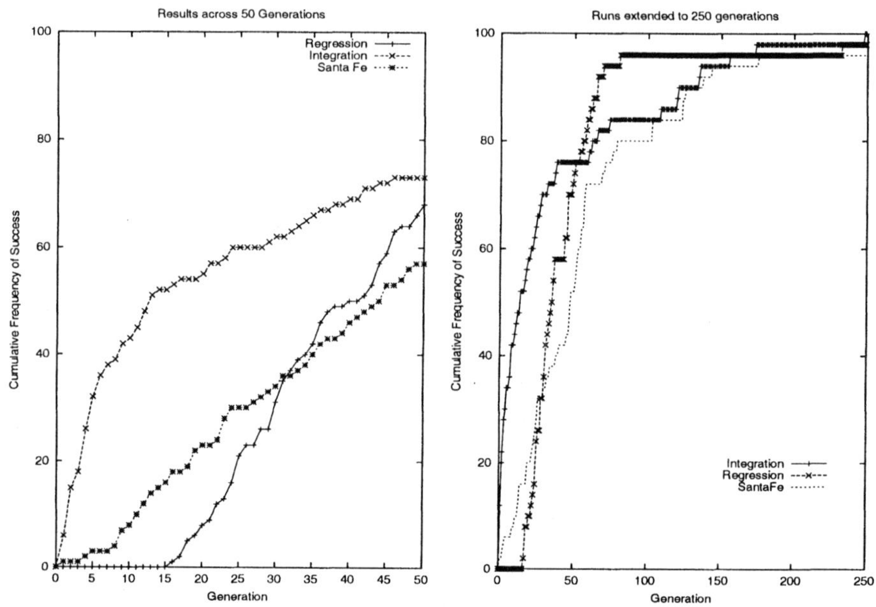

Figure 8.4. Left : The performance of Chorus at 50 generations. Right : The performance at 250 generations.

The next choice is between rules #C and #D, however, as #D already has a positive concentration, the system does not read any more codons from the chromosome, and instead uses the values present. As a result, rule `<var> -> X` is chosen to introduce first terminal symbol in the expression.

Once this non-terminal has been mapped to a terminal, we move to the next left most terminal, `<op>` and carry on from there. If, while reading the genome, we come to the end, and and there is still a tie between 2 or more rules, the one that appears first in the concentration table is chosen. However if concentrations of all the relevant rules is zero, the mapping terminates and the individual responsible is given a suitably chastening fitness.

With this particular individual, mapping continues, till the individual is completely mapped. The mapped individual is

```
X * X + ( X * X ).
```

5.2 RESULTS

Initial experiments with Chorus have indicated that it is initially slower at evolving solutions than either GE or GP, but does reach the same levels of fitness. Typical performance comparisons are like those in Figure 8.4 which shows how well Chorus succeeds at solving three problems. The graph on the right indicate how much performance increases when the runs are extended, which is roughly the same as both GE and GP.

The slow start for Chorus may, however, be an advantage, as research has indicated that Chorus maintains a considerably more diverse population than the other methods. The cost of this, of course, is slower evolution.

6. FINANCIAL PREDICTION

Recently Grammatical Evolution has been successfully applied to a number of problems broadly encompassed by the area of financial prediction.

These include the prediction of corporate failure (Brabazon et al., 2002a), modelling the relationship between corporate strategy and financial performance (Brabazon et al., 2002b) and the automatic generation of trading rules for both market indices and foreign exchange markets (O'Neill et al., 2001b; O'Neill et al., 2001a; O'Neill et al., 2002; Brabazon and O'Neill, 2002). In the case of generating trading rules for financial markets, the only change required to Grammatical Evolution was the writing of a grammar that allowed the generation of syntactically correct trading rules, all other system parameters were left unmodified in their standard settings. What follows is a sample of this work demonstrating the automatic generation of trading rules for market indices.

6.1 TRADING MARKET INDICES

A market index is comprised of a weighted average measure of the price of individual shares which make up that market. The value of the index represents an aggregation of the balance of supply and demand for these shares. Some market traders, technical analysts, believe that prices move in trends and that price patterns repeat themselves (Murphy, 1999). If we accept the premise that there are rules, although not necessarily static rules, underlying price behaviour, it follows that trading decisions could be enhanced through use of an appropriate rule induction methodology such as Grammatical Evolution (GE).

The development of trading rules based on current and historic market price information has a long history (Brown et al., 1998). The process entails the selection of one or more technical indicators and the development of a trading system based on these indicators. These indicators are formed from various combinations of current and historic price information. Although there are potentially an infinite number of such indicators, the financial literature suggests that certain indicators are widely used by investors (Brock et al., 1992)(Murphy, 1999) (Pring, 1991).

Four groupings of indicators are given prominence in prior literature:

i. Moving average indicators

ii. Momentum indicators

iii. Trading range indicators

iv. Oscillators

Given the large search space, an evolutionary automatic programming methodology has promise to determine both a good quality combination of, and relevant parameters for, trading rules drawn from individual technical indicators. For the experiments reported here moving average, momentum, and trading range volatility indicators are used.

The rules evolved by GE are used to generate one of three signals for each day of the training or test periods. The possible signals are *Buy*, *Sell*, or *Do Nothing*. Permitting the model to output a Do Nothing signal reduces the hard threshold problem associated with production of a binary output. This issue has not been considered in a number of prior studies. A variant on the trading methodology developed in Brock et al. (Brock et al., 1992) is then applied.

If a buy signal is indicated, a fixed investment of $1,000 (arbitrary) is made in the market index. This position is closed at the end of a ten day (arbitrary) period.

On the production of a sell signal, an investment of $1,000 is sold short and again this position is closed out after a ten day period. This gives rise to a maximum potential investment of $10,000 at any point in time (the potential loss on individual short sales is in theory infinite but in practice is unlikely to exceed $1,000).

In addition to the technical indicators the grammar (given below) also allows the use of the binary operators `f_and`, `f_or`, the standard arithmetic operators, and the unary operator `f_not`, and the current days index value `day`. The operations `f_and`, `f_or`, and `f_not` return the minimum, maximum, of the arguments, and 1 - the argument, respectively.

```
N={<code>,<expr>,<fopbi>,<fopun>,<matbi>,<relbi>,<var>,<int>}
T={p,=,(,),f_and,f_or,f_not,+,-,*,>,<,>=,<=,scale,ma,day,1,2,3,4,5,10}
S=<code>
P={ <code> ::=  p = <expr> ;

<expr> ::= <fopbi> (<expr>, <expr>) | <fopun> (<expr>) | <expr><matbi><expr>
         | <expr><relbi><expr> | <var>

<fopbi> ::= f_and | f_or

<fopun> ::= f_not

<matbi> ::= + | - | *

<relbi> ::= > | < | >= | <=

<var> ::= <int> | day | ma(<int>,day) | momentum(<int>,day)  | trb(<int>,day)

<int> ::= 1 | 2 | 3 | 4 | 5 | 10 }
```

The signals generated for each day, Buy, Sell, or Do Nothing, are post-processed using fuzzy logic. We use pre-determined membership functions, in this case, to determine what the meaning of this value is. The membership functions adopted were as follows:

$$Buy = Value < .33$$
$$DoNothing = .33 >= Value < .66$$
$$Sell = .66 >= Value$$

A key decision in applying an EAP methodology to construct a technical trading system is to determine what fitness measure should be adopted. A simple fitness measure such as the profitability of the system both in and out of sample is inadequate as it fails to consider the risk associated with the developed trading system. The risk of the system can be estimated in a variety of ways. One possibility is to consider market risk, defined here as the risk of loss of funds due to a market movement. A measure of this risk is provided by the maximum drawdown (maximum cumulative loss) of the system during a training or test period. This measure of risk can be incorporated into the fitness function in a variety of formats including: (return/maximum drawdown) or return - 'x'(maximum drawdown), where 'x' is a pre-determined constant dependent on an investor's psychological risk profile. For a given rate of return, the system generating the lowest maximum drawdown is preferred.

This study incorporates drawdown in the fitness function by subtracting the maximum cumulative loss during the training period from the profit generated during that period. This is a conservative approach which will encourage the evolution of trading systems with good return to risk characteristics. This will provide a more stringent test of trading rule performance as high risk/high reward trading rules will be discriminated against.

6.1.1 EXPERIMENTAL SETUP & RESULTS

The data sets used are the daily data for the UK FTSE 100, the German DAX, and the Japanese NIKKEI stock indices. The values of the indices changed substantially over the training and testing period. Before the trading rules were constructed, these values were normalised using a two phase preprocessing. Initially the daily values were transformed by dividing them by a 75 day lagged moving average. These transformed values are then normalised using linear scaling into the range 0 to 1. This procedure is a variant on that adopted by (Allen and Karjalainen, 1999) and (Iba and Nikolaev, 2000).

The FTSE data is drawn from the period 26/04/1984 to 4/12/1997, the training data set was comprised of 365 days from the first day plus an additional 75 days at the beginning of this time to allow for the time lag introduced with technical indicators such as the moving average. The remaining data is divided into five hold out samples totaling 2125 trading days. The DAX and NIKKEI data are drawn from the period 01/01/1991 to 03/12/1997, with the initial 440 days becoming the training data set as before. The remaining data is divided into two hold out samples in each case.

The division of the hold out period into a number of segments is undertaken to allow comparison of the out of sample results across different market conditions, in order to assess the stability and degradation characteristics of the developed model's predictions.

The profit (or loss) on each transaction is calculated taking into account a one-way trading cost of 0.2% and allowing a further 0.3% for slippage. The total return generated by the developed trading system is a combination of its trading return and its risk free rate of return generated on uncommitted funds.

The rate adopted in this calculation is simplified to be the average interest rate over the entire data set. For the FTSE the rate is 8.5%, the DAX 6.0% and for the NIKKEI it is 1.5%.

Thirty runs were performed on each of the three datasets using a population size of 500 individuals over 100 generations. Bit mutation at a probability of 0.01, and a variable-length one-point crossover probability of 0.9 was adopted. A comparison of the best individuals evolved for each dataset to the benchmark buy and hold strategy can be seen in Table 8.7, Table 8.8, and Table 8.9, for the FTSE, DAX and NIKKEI datasets respectively.

Table 8.7. A comparison of the buy and hold benchmark to the best evolved individual for the FTSE dataset.

Trading Period (Days)	*Buy & Hold Profit (US$)*	*Best-of-run Profit(US$)*	*Best-of-run Avg. Daily Investment*
Train (75 to 440)	3071	3156	3219
Test 1 (440 to 805)	5244	1607	1822
Test 2 (805 to 1170)	-1376	4710	3151
Test 3 (1170 to 1535)	1979	2387	6041
Test 4 (1535 to 1900)	1568	-173	3274
Test 5 (3196 to 3552)	3200	2221	3767
Total	13686	13908	

Table 8.8. A comparison of the benchmark buy and hold strategy to the best evolved individual on the DAX dataset.

Trading Period (Days)	*Buy & Hold Profit (US$)*	*Best-of-run Profit(US$)*	*Best-of-run Avg. Daily Investment*
Train (440 to 805)	3835	3648	7548
Test 1 (805 to 1170)	-41	-1057	8178
Test 2 (1170 to 1535)	3016	469	8562
Total	6831	3060	

Table 8.9. A comparison of the benchmark buy and hold strategy to the best evolved individual on the NIKKEI dataset.

Trading Period (Days)	*Buy & Hold Profit (US$)*	*Best-of-run Profit(US$)*	*Best-of-run Avg. Daily Investment*
Train (75 to 440)	-6285	3227	9247
Test 1 (440 to 805)	59	-1115	7164
Test 2 (805 to 1170)	-3824	633	9192
Total	-10050	2745	

In the case of the FTSE and NIKKEI datasets the evolved rules produce a superior performance to the benchmark strategy, while performance over the DAX dataset is not as strong. The poorer performance for the DAX market can be attributed to over-fitting of the evolved rules to the training data. For each of the evolved trading rules the associated risk is less than that of the benchmark strategy as can be seen in the average daily investment figures reported.

7. ADAPTIVE LOGIC PROGRAMMING

Logic Programming (Burke and Foxley, 1996) makes a rigorous distinction between the declarative aspect of a computer program and the procedural part. The declarative part defines everything that is 'true' in the specific domain, while the procedural part derives instances of these 'truths'.

The programming language Prolog (Sterling and Shapiro, 1994) fills in the procedural aspect by employing a strict depth-first search-strategy through the rules (clauses) defined by a logic program. With Adaptive Logic Programming (ALP), GE is used as an alternative search strategy.

Prolog is a useful target language because of its support for the specification of constraints, which can be anything from the size of the program, to the use of certain terminals, to the support for multiple types.

7.1 LOGIC PROGRAMMING

A logic program consists of clauses consisting of a head and a body. In Prolog notation, identifiers starting with an uppercase character are considered to be logic variables, while lowercase characters are atoms or function symbols. The logic program

```
sym(x).
sym(y).
sym(X + Y) :- sym(X), sym(Y).
sym(X * Y) :- sym(X), sym(Y).
```

defines a single predicate *sym*. The derivation symbol *:-/2* should be read as an inverse implication sign. In predicate logic the third *clause* can then be interpreted as

$$\forall X, Y : sym(X) \wedge sym(Y) \rightarrow sym(X + Y)$$

The query

```
?- sym(X).
```

can be interpreted as the inquiry $\exists X : sym(X)$[3] and produces in Prolog the following sequence of solutions:

```
X = x;
X = y;
X = x + x;
X = x + y;
X = x + (x + x);
X = x + (x + y);
X = x + (x + (x + x));
...
```

Extrapolating this sequence it is easy to see that without bounds on the depth or size of the derivation, the depth-first clause selection with backtracking strategy employed in Prolog will never generate an expression that contains the multiplication character. Therefore, while the depth-first selection of clauses may be *sound*, it is not *complete* w.r.t. an arbitrary logic program[4].

Logic programming is a convenient paradigm for specifying languages and constraints. A predicate can have several *attributes* and these attributes can be used to constrain the search space. For example, the logic program and query

```
sym(x,1).
sym(y,1).
sym(X+Y,S) :-
   sym(X,S1), sym(Y,S2), S is S1+S2+1.
sym(X*Y,S) :-
   sym(X,S1), sym(Y,S2), S is S1+S2+1.

?-sym(X, S), S<10.
```

[3]Formally the negation of this formula is disproven, thus proving this formula.

[4]A depth-first strategy is however far more efficient than the breadth-first alternative

specifies all expressions of size smaller than 10. With such terse yet powerful descriptiveness, it is therefore no surprise that attribute logic and constraint logic programming are more often than not implemented in Prolog. It is this convenient representation of data or program structures together with constraints that we are trying to exploit.

Formally, a Logic Programming system is defined by Selected Literal Definite clause resolution (or SLD-resolution for short), and an *oracle* function that selects the next clause or the next literal[5]. This *oracle* function is in Prolog implemented as:

- Select first clause
- Select first literal
- Backtrack on failure

7.2 GE AND LOGIC PROGRAMMING

In this work we similarly use a sequence of choices as the base representation, but rather than choosing between the production rules of a context-free grammar, they are used to make a choice between clauses in a logic program. The sequence of choices thus represents one part of the selection function operating together with SLD-resolution on the logic program. Furthermore, backtracking is implemented in the system together with an alternative strategy on failure: restarting the original query.

As an example of the mapping process, consider the grammar defined above in Section 7.1, and an evolutionary induced sequence of choices $[2, 1, 3, 0, 1]$. The derivation of an instance then proceeds as follows:

```
?- sym(X).
?- sym(X1), sym(X2). [(X1 + X2)/X]  2
?- sym(y),  sym(X2). [y/X1]         1
?- sym(X3), sym(X4). [(X3 * X4)/X2] 3
?- sym(x),  sym(X4). [x/X3]         0
?- sym(y).           [y/X4]         1
```

Applying all bindings made produces the symbolic expression: $y+x*y$. The values from the sequence of choices are in this example conveniently chosen to lie between 0 and 3 inclusive; in practice a number encountered in the genotype can be higher than the number of choices present. The choice will then be taken modulo the number of available choices.

[5] A literal is a single predicate call in the body of a clause or query. In the query above, $sym(X, S)$ and $S < 10$ are literals.

In this example, the depth-first clause selection of Prolog is replaced by a guided selection where choices are drawn from the genotype. The first unresolved literal is still chosen to be the first to derive. It is possible to replace this with guided selection as well, be it in the same string or in a separate string. Together with a choice whether to do backtracking or not, this leads to Table 8.10 which gives an overview of the parts of the Prolog engine that can be replaced. Table 8.10 thus defines a family of adaptive logic programming systems. Enumerating them, ALP-0 will correspond with a Prolog system, while ALP-1 (modified clause selection) and ALP-4 (modified clause selection without backtracking) correspond with the systems examined here.

Table 8.10. The possible modifications to the selection function.

Selection	*Prolog*	*Modification*
Clause	First Found	From Genotype
Literal	First Found	From Genotype
On Failure	Backtrack	Restart

This work has chosen to focus on ALP-1 and ALP-4 as there are some practical problems associated with replacing literal selection. In many applications, a logic program consists of a mix of non-deterministic predicates (such as the *sym/1 and sym/2* predicates above) and deterministic predicates (such as the assignment function *is/2*). The deterministic predicates often assume some variables to be bound to ground terms, evaluating them out of order would then lead to runtime exceptions.

A logic program is thus used as a formal specification of the language, the sequence of choices is used to steer the resolution process and a small external program is used to evaluate the expressions generated. The scope of the system are then logic programs where there is an abundance of solutions that satisfy the constraints, which are subsequently evaluated for performance on a problem domain.

7.2.1 BACKTRACKING

In ALP-1, at every step in the derivation process, a list is maintained of clauses that are not tried yet. When a query fails at a certain point, the selection function will be asked to pick a new choice out of the remaining clauses. This choice is removed and when all are exhausted, the branch reports failure to the previous level where this procedure starts again.

ALP-4 does not use backtracking; on failure it will restart the original, top-level, query, while the reading continues from where it left of.

If the sequence runs out of choices, i.e., the end of the genotype is reached, the derivation is cut off and the individual gets the worst performance value available. This will be labelled a failure.

7.2.2 INITIALISATION

Initialisation is performed by doing a random walk through the grammar, maintaining the choices made, backtracking on failure (ALP-1) or restarting (ALP-4). After a successful derivation is found, the shortest, non-backtracking path to the complete derivation is calculated. An occurrence check is performed and if the path is not present in the current population, a new individual is initialised with this shortest non-backtracking path. Individuals in the initial population will thus consist solely of non-backtracking derivations to sentences. Typically a depth limit is employed.

7.3 DISCUSSION

The system presented here is the first prototype for evolving sentences in languages with constraints, and has been shown to be able to optimize a range of standard problems (Keijzer et al., 2001a), including a difficult language such as the units of measurement grammar.

The initialisation procedure as is described here does not provide an optimal starting point for the ALP systems. The initialisation procedure consists of non-backtracking points to derivations, with no unexpressed code. It is an avenue of future research to find a better initialisation procedure. However, the highly explorative nature of the crossover used here, enables the system to overcome this and even with a non-optimal starting point, it is able to find competitive solutions to the problems presented to it.

The main benefit of the ALPs system in contrast with strongly typed genetic programming systems is that the variational operators do not depend as heavily on the grammar that is used. A strongly typed crossover is constrained to search in the space of available types in the population, thus having a strong macro-mutation flavor (Angeline, 1997). The ALP systems, borrowing the mapping process from Grammatical Evolution, is in principle not thus constrained. New instances of types can be created during the run.

Subsequent work (Keijzer, 2002) has shown that ALP is particularly suited to symbolic regression problems, problems requiring context-sensitive constraints and problems that require dimensions.

8. SENSIBLE INITIALISATION

One of the key characteristics of Evolutionary Algorithms is the manner in which solutions are evolved from a primordial soup. The way this soup, or initial generation, is created can have major implications for the eventual quality of the search, as, if there is not enough diversity, the population may become stuck on a local optimum.

The quality of solution produced by a system can be related to the quality of the initial generation. In particular, if the initial generation contains a large number of invalid individuals, the effective size of the pool can be drastically reduced. As discussed in chapter 5, this can often happen with GE, with initial populations often showing over 70% invalid individuals.

This is due to the entirely random manner in which the individuals in the first population are generated. Unlike initialisation in GP, there is no guarantee that the individuals created will actually map to completion, as the codons are generated without respect to their predecessors.

GP has a variety of initialisation methods, the most common of which is *ramped half-and-half*, as described in chapter 6. Some of these are *smart* initialisation methods, in that they try to incorporate some useful information into the population, such as previous solutions, or domain specific knowledge. Other methods, on the other hand, are merely what we term *sensible*, in that they only attempt to make the initial population as general as possible.

It is a relatively simple task to employ a type of sensible initialisation in GE which is analogous to the ramped half and half method described by Koza. In Koza's GP, functions are responsible for the growth of a tree. As GE uses grammars, this role is taken over by the *recursive* production rules. We define a rule to be recursive due to three reasons.

- The right hand side of the production rule may contain the non-terminal on the left hand side.
- The right hand side of a rule may contain a non-terminal which points to a rule that is recursive due to any of the other two reasons.
- The right hand side of a rule may contain a non-terminal that leads back to the same production rule. Consider the mutually recursive rules given below.

```
<line>       ::= <condition>
<condition> ::= if(trail.food_ahead())
                  { <line> } else { <line> }
```

`<line>` leads to the non-terminal `<condition>`, which in turn takes us back to `<line>`. This labels both the rules as recursive. We also calculate the minimum depth required by a production rule to lead to all terminal symbols. Consider the grammar given below where S is the start symbol.

```
S=<expr>
<expr>    ::=  <expr> <op> <expr>   (0)
```

```
                | <var>                   (1)
<op>        ::= +                         (2)
<var>       ::= X                         (3)
```

Consider rule 0 from the grammar. Non-terminal `<op>` maps directly to terminals, thus its minimum depth is 2. `<expr>` on the other hand first maps to rule 1, which in turn takes one more step to map to the terminal symbol employing rule 3, thus requiring a minimum depth of 3. As rule 0 involves both `<op>` and `<expr>`, the maximum of the minimum depths of the two non-terminals, i.e., 3, is the minimum depth for rule 0.

Once these two parameters have been noted for every rule, i.e., the recursive nature and the minimum depth, we can generate derivation trees in the manner similar to ramped half and half for Koza's GP. Whenever the tree has to be grown, only those productions are chosen from, whose minimum depth is less than or equal to the remaining allowed depth. This is calculated by subtracting the tree's current depth from the maximum allowed depth. If we are using the full method, if possible, we only choose recursive rules. In case of grow, recursive and non-recursive rules are chosen with equal probability.

This is a very inexpensive way to generate trees, as no effort is made to encode any kind of problem specific information in them, and no test is done to determine if two trees are functionally identical which, given that trees of different shapes can be functionally identical could be a very expensive exercise. A simple clone check can be carried out by comparing the linear chromosomes, however, to determine if two individuals have made exactly the same choices. Again, this is a very cheap operation, as comparisons only have to be made against individuals of identical length.

Initial results suggest that Sensible Initialisation improves the performance of GE, by providing a far greater diversity than random initialisation.

9. GENETIC PROGRAMMING

As indicated in chapter 7, even Genetic Programming uses a grammar. Although many GP users may be surprised to hear this claim, a function and terminal set implicitly describes a grammar; one indicates the arity of the functions and, as every function can take every terminal as well as the output of every function, it is simply a matter adhering to the arity demands of every function to produce legal programs.

The arity of the functions could easily be described by a CFG. Consider the GP function and terminal set

$$F = \{+, *, -, \%\}, T = \{x, y\}$$

Where each of the four functions have an arity of two. This could also be described by the Context Free Grammar (CFG):

```
E ::= x | y | (+ E E)|(* E E)|(- E E)|(% E E)
```

where E is the start symbol.

This kind of CFG differs from the standard type only in that there is a single non-terminal. The use of a single non-terminal implies that the grammar has the closure property, so desirous of the GP crossover operator. Notice that use of more than one non-terminal does not preclude a grammar from being closed. The question of its closure can only be resolved by determining if it can be rewritten as an equivalent grammar with a single non-terminal.

Crossover is considered to be the driving force behind GP, and the crossover used by GE has been identified as *ripple* crossover. To convert GE to the sub-tree crossover used by GP, one simply needs to perform a restricted form of two point crossover. Two point crossover is required because we need to emulate sub-tree crossover to correctly implement GP.

Due to the restricted form of the grammar, individuals using this grammar effectively code prefix expressions, which have been shown (Keith and Martin, 1994) to be a particularly efficient way to store GP (and evaluate) individuals. They demonstrated a simple algorithm to perform subtree crossover on these types of individuals.

To identify the end of a subtree, one proceeds from the root note (selected randomly for crossover), taking the arity of each node minus one, and summing them. For example, for the subtree $(+\ x\ y)$, one would initially start with a total of one. That is, the arity of $+$ (two) minus one. The arity of each of the terminals is zero, so by the time we reach y, the total is minus one, indicating the end of the subtree.

When performing crossover, one simply selects two subtrees from each individual using the above method, and swapping them with each other. If the space vacated by each isn't the correct size for the other, one simply grows or shrinks the space as required. The closed nature of the grammar used for this will ensure that individuals produced in this way will always be legal.

10. CONCLUSIONS

The ideas and work presented here demonstrate the power of flexibility that Grammatical Evolution provides, and yet we merely scratch the surface of extensions and applications that are possible. The modular design of Grammatical Evolution allows us to radically change the manner in which the algorithm behaves by merely changing the grammar supplied, and allows us to benefit from the latest advances in evolutionary algorithm research by updating the search engine used to manipulate an individual. In the next chapter we go on to outline what directions we envisage research in this area may take.

Chapter 9

CONCLUSIONS & FUTURE WORK

1. SUMMARY

We have presented Grammatical Evolution (GE), a system that is capable of evolving computer programs in an arbitrary language. This ability is achieved through the adoption of a genotype-phenotype distinction, that generates the output program by the application of production rules from a grammar. The grammar is used to specify the output language and its syntax, therefore allowing program generation in any language. A number of additional features inspired by Molecular Biology are achieved. These include: a separation of the search and solution spaces that allow the EA search engine to be a plug-in component of the system, facilitating the exploitation of advances in EA's by GE; a many-to-one, degenerate genetic code that allows the exploitation of neutral evolution to enhance the search efficiency of the EA; and the use of a wrapping operator, that allows the reuse of genetic material during a genotype-phenotype mapping process.

Following from a review of Automatic Programming in which the focus of attention was drawn towards Evolutionary Automatic Programming, we examined a number of potential advantages that could be achieved through a genotype-phenotype distinction in chapter 3, and later showed evidence of their existence in GE in chapters 4 and 6. The ability of this approach to evolve computer programs using proof of concept problems was demonstrated in chapter 5, with the performance of GE shown to be on a par with, and in some cases superior to, Genetic Programming.

An analysis of GE was conducted in chapters 6 and 7 and a number of interesting results were obtained. It was found that the novel wrapping operator was useful in promoting the completion of successful genotype-phenotype mappings, and that some compression of the genotype was observed. The degenerate genetic code was found to have desirable features, such as maintenance of genetic diversity within the population, an improvement in the success rate of runs, and a preservation of the functionality of evolving programs whilst the evolutionary search is still being conducted. A detailed analysis of crossover in GE determined that the one-point crossover adopted has a dramatic positive effect on the performance of the system. This effect, we suggest, is due to the global search that is conducted by virtue of its mechanism that becomes apparent when examined in terms of parse trees, by swapping on average half of the genetic material.

Chapter 8 saw a description of some of our more recent investigations into extensions and applications of GE, however, most of what was presented is in early stages of development. The following section speaks about these and other open issues for GE. To keep up to date with the latest on GE please refer to the grammatical-evolution.org website (GE., 2003).

2. FUTURE WORK

Various questions are posed as a result of the body of work presented in this book, and many avenues of investigation have yet to be explored. The following is a list of possible lines of research that could be profitable to GE and to the Evolutionary Automatic Programming community at large.

The Grammar.

The grammar adopted by GE is a context-free grammar that is used to ensure the syntactic correctness of the evolving programs. The next step in the development of GE would be to investigate the use of context sensitive, attribute and logic grammars. These grammars extend the expressive power of a context-free grammar by taking into account semantic information, and the context of the current non-terminal in the code as it is being generated. These context-sensitive grammars would allow the incorporation of information on types, facilitating the evolution of multi-typed programs.

The grammar could also be used as a mechanism to incorporate an equivalent of the automatically defined functions of Genetic Programming. Some initial investigations with encouraging results have been conducted in (O'Neill and Ryan, 2000). This approach will come into its own when it is possible to dynamically change the grammar used during the mapping process of GE. This will enable dynamic automatic function definition where the number and type of functions no longer has to be pre-determined, but rather would be evolved.

No effort has been made during the course of the research presented here to conduct an analysis of different grammars and their effects on the performance of GE. During the experiments we have conducted, very simple, tailored grammars were adopted. It is possible to include the entire grammar for a language such as C into this system, or indeed to use different variations on the grammars that we have adopted. As noted in (Whigham, 1996a) it is possible to use the grammar to incorporate bias into the evolutionary search. It is therefore, necessary to discover what effects different grammars would have on GE. Through the adoption of dynamic grammars that are open to the processes of evolution it would be possible to co-evolve the grammar with the solution it represents. This would allow language bias to be learnt, and open to adaptation.

Transcription Model.

The manner in which the genome is read and converted into codon integer values is a very simplistic transcription process model. Many potential avenues of investigation are possible with this model. One example would include the investigation of different wrapping strategies, for example, using different reading frames after a wrap event. More complex models such as the operon model (as described in chapter 3) might be implemented.

The incorporation of introns into GE through a mechanism like grammar defined introns (see chapter 8) is another area that might have benefits. Conflicting reports exist on the benefit or otherwise of introns in evolutionary computation, and, as such, it would be interesting to test their effects on GE.

Translation Model.

Throughout the course of this work the mapping function that comprises the translation model of GE has remained static. The mapping function

$$Rule = (Codon\ value)\ MOD\ (Number\ of\ choices)$$

has proven to be a powerful component of GE being responsible for the intrinsic polymorphism properties that can arise during crossover events (see chapter 7). It would be interesting to explore variations on the translation model with the use of different mapping functions. Initial investigations have begun in this area with the bucket rule, as described in chapter 8.

In conjunction with the grammar (grammar co-evolution) it would also be possible to test the effects of evolving the genetic code on-line.

The Evolutionary Algorithm Engine.

For the sake of simplicity we have adopted a simple GA for the proof of concept problems and system analysis. As the scalability of the simple GA to harder problems has been shown to be poor, it would be useful to study the benefits of the so-called competent GAs (GAs with improved scaling characteristics) on the scalability of GE(Goldberg, 2002).

Other modifications to the evolutionary algorithm engine could include concepts such as diploidy and polygenic inheritance, particularly if the system was to be applied to dynamic problem domains.

Some investigations into the use of alternatives for evolutionary-based search strategies have begun, as described in chapter 8. Given that the search component of GE is a plug-in, it is easy to adopt search strategies that can manipulate binary or integer strings.

The Initialisation Strategy.

The creation of generation zero has been a purely random approach up until now. As alternative intialisation strategies are found to be of benefit to GP, the investigation of similar strategies in GE may yield efficiency gains. Further experimentation using the sensible initialisation procedure described in the last chapter must be undertaken.

Neutral Evolution.

No analysis has been conducted on the evolutionary dynamics during this work, but we have speculated on the exploitation of neutral evolution by GE. In order to determine if we are benefiting from neutral evolutionary processes, further investigations must be conducted. We are particularly interested in adopting visualisation techniques that are being used to give insights into the dynamics of other evolutionary algorithms.

Application Areas.

One of the major steps forward will be the application of GE to real-world problems. We demonstrated success with GE's application to some standard benchmark problems and a real-world caching algorithm problem in chapter 5, and in addition with the diverse applications presented in chapter 8. The flexibility of GE in its ability to produce programs in an arbitrary language will facilitate its application to many different problem domains. According to the No Free Lunch theorem, GE won't be optimal at all problems, but it would be interesting to determine for what classes of problems this type of Evolutionary Automatic Programming system is useful.

References

Allen, F. and Karjalainen, R. (1999). Using genetic algorithms to find technical trading rules. *Journal of Financial Economics*, 54:245–271.

Altenberg, L. (1994). The evolution of evolvability in genetic programming. In Kinnear, Jr., K. E., editor, *Advances in Genetic Programming*, chapter 3, pages 47–74. MIT Press.

Andre, D. and Teller, A. (1996). A study in program response and the negative effects of introns in genetic programming. In Koza, J. R., Goldberg, D. E., Fogel, D. B., and Riolo, R. L., editors, *Genetic Programming 1996: Proceedings of the First Annual Conference*, pages 12–20, Stanford University, CA, USA. MIT Press.

Angeline, P. J. (1994). Genetic programming and emergent intelligence. In Kinnear, Jr., K. E., editor, *Advances in Genetic Programming*, chapter 4, pages 75–98. MIT Press.

Angeline, P. J. (1997). Subtree crossover: Building block engine or macromutation? In Koza, J. R., Deb, K., Dorigo, M., Fogel, D. B., Garzon, M., Iba, H., and Riolo, R. L., editors, *Genetic Programming 1997: Proceedings of the Second Annual Conference*, pages 9–17, Stanford University, CA, USA. Morgan Kaufmann.

Angeline, P. J. and Kinnear, Jr., K. E., editors (1996). *Advances in Genetic Programming 2*. MIT Press, Cambridge, MA, USA.

Azad, R. M. A., Ryan, C., Burke, M. E., and Ansari, A. R. (2002). A re-examination of the cart centering problem using the chorus system. In Langdon, W. B., Cantú-Paz, E., Mathias, K., Roy, R., Davis, D., Poli, R., Balakrishnan, K., Honavar, V., Rudolph, G., Wegener, J., Bull, L., Potter, M. A., Schultz, A. C., Miller, J. F., Burke, E., and Jonoska, N., editors, *GECCO 2002: Proceedings of the Genetic and Evolutionary Computation Conference*, pages 707–715, New York. Morgan Kaufmann Publishers.

Backus, J. W., Wegstein, J. H., van Wijngaarden, A., Woodger, M., Bauer, F. L., Green, J., Katz, C., McCarthy, J., Perlis, A. J., Rutishauser, H., Samelson, K., and Vauquois, B. (1960). Report on the algorithmic language algol 60. *Communications of the ACM*, 3(5):299–314.

Banzhaf, W. (1994). Genotype-phenotype-mapping and neutral variation – A case study in genetic programming. In Davidor, Y., Schwefel, H.-P., and Männer, R., editors, *Parallel Problem Solving from Nature III*, pages 322–332, Jerusalem. Springer-Verlag.

Banzhaf, W., Nordin, P., Keller, R. E., and Francone, F. D. (1998). *Genetic Programming – An Introduction; On the Automatic Evolution of Computer Programs and its Applications*. Morgan Kaufmann, dpunkt.verlag.

Barnett, L. (1997). Evolutionary dynamics on fitness landscapes with neutrality. Master's thesis, School of Cognitive Sciences, University of East Sussex, Brighton.

Barreau, G. (2000). *The Evolutionary Consequences of Redundancy in Natural and Artificial Genetic Codes*. PhD thesis, University of Sussex.

Bernier, J. L. and Herraiz, C. I. (1996). Solving mastermind using gas and simulated annealing: a case of dynamic constraint optimization. In *Proceedings of PPSN, Parallel Problem Solving from Nature IV*.

Blume, W. and Eigenmann, R. (1992). Performance analysis pf parallelizing compilers on the Perfect Benchmarks programs. *IEEE Transactions on Parallel and Distributed Systems*, 3(6):643–656.

Brabazon, A., O'Neill, M., Matthews, R., and Ryan, C. (2002a). Grammatical evolution and corporate failure prediction. In Langdon, W. B., Cantú-Paz, E., Mathias, K., Roy, R., Davis, D., Poli, R., Balakrishnan, K., Honavar, V., Rudolph, G., Wegener, J., Bull, L., Potter, M. A., Schultz, A. C., Miller, J. F., Burke, E., and Jonoska, N., editors, *GECCO 2002: Proceedings of the Genetic and Evolutionary Computation Conference*, pages 1011–1018, New York. Morgan Kaufmann Publishers.

Brabazon, A., O'Neill, M., Ryan, C., and Matthews, R. (2002b). Evolving classifiers to model the relationship between strategy and corporate performance using grammatical evolution. In Lutton, E., Foster, J. A., Miller, J., Ryan, C., and Tettamanzi, A. G. B., editors, *Proceedings of the 4th European Conference on Genetic Programming, EuroGP 2002*, volume 2278 of *LNCS*, pages 103–112, Kinsale, Ireland. Springer-Verlag.

Brabazon, T. and O'Neill, M. (2002). Trading foreign exchange markets using evolutionary automatic programming. In Barry, A. M., editor, *GECCO 2002: Proceedings of the Bird of a Feather Workshops, Genetic and Evolutionary Computation Conference*, pages 133–136, New York. AAAI.

Brock, W., Lakonishok, J., and LeBaron, B. (1992). Simple technical trading rules and the stochastic properties of stock returns. *Journal of Finance*, 47(5):1731–1764.

Brown, S., Goetzmann, W., and Kumar, A. (1998). The dow theory: William peter hamilton's track record reconsidered. *Journal of Finance*, 53(4):1311–1333.

Burke, E. and Foxley, E. (1996). *Logic and Its Applications*. Prentice Hall.

Chomsky, N. (1956). Three models for the description of language. *IEEE Transactions on Information Theory*, 2(3):113–124.

Collins, J. and Ryan, C. (1999). Non-stationary function optimization using polygenic inheritance. In Banzhaf, W., Daida, J., Eiben, A. E., Garzon, M. H., Honavar, V., Jakiela, M., and Smith, R. E., editors, *Proceedings of the Genetic and Evolutionary Computation Conference*, volume 1, page 781, Orlando, Florida, USA. Morgan Kaufmann.

Collins, R. (1992). *Studies in Artificial Life*. PhD thesis, University of California, Los Angeles.

Cramer, N. L. (1985). A representation for the adaptive generation of simple sequential programs. In Grefenstette, J. J., editor, *Proceedings of the International Conference on Genetic Algorithms and Their Applications*, pages 183–187, Carnegie-Mellon University, Pittsburgh, PA.

Crick, F. (1966). Codon-anticodon pairing; the wobble hypothesis. *Journal of Molecular Biology*, 19:548–555.

Darwin, C. (1859). *On the Origins of the Species by Means of Natural Selection, or the Preservation of Favoured Races in the Struggle for Life*.

De Jong, K. (1999). *Evolutionary Algorithms in Engineering and Computer Science*, chapter 3. Evolutionary Computation: Recent Developments and Open Issues, pages 43–54. Wiley.

Deb, K. and Goldberg, D. (1991). mga in c: A messy genetic algorithm in c. Technical Report 91008, Illinois Genetic Algorithms Laboratory (IlliGAL).

Eigen, M., Caskill, J. M., and Schuster, P. (1989). The molecular quasispecies. *Adv. Chem. Phys.*, 75:149–263.

Engelhardt, R. (1998). *Emergent Percolating Nets in Evolution*. PhD thesis, Center for Chaos and Turbulence Studies, Univeristy of Copenhagen.

Erik van Nimwegen, J. P. C. (1999). Metastable evolutionary dymnamics: Crossing fitness barriers or escaping via neutral paths? Technical Report 99-07-041, Santa Fe Institute.

Flanagan, K., Grimsrud, K., Archibald, J., and Nelson, B. (1992). Bach: Byu address collection hardware. Technical Report TR-A150-92.1., Electrical and Computer Engineering Department, Brigham Young University.

Fogel, L., Owens, A., and Walsh, M. (1966). *Artificial Intelligence through Simulated Evolution*. John Wiley.

Foster, I. (1991). Automatic generation of self-scheduling programs. *IEEE Transactions on Parallel and Distributed Systems*, 2(1):68–78.

Francone, F. D., Conrads, M., Banzhaf, W., and Nordin, P. (1999). Homologous crossover in genetic programming. In Banzhaf, W., Daida, J., Eiben, A. E., Garzon, M. H., Honavar, V., Jakiela, M., and Smith, R. E., editors, *Proceedings of the Genetic and Evolutionary Computation Conference*, volume 2, pages 1021–1026, Orlando, Florida, USA. Morgan Kaufmann.

Francone, F. D., Nordin, P., and Banzhaf, W. (1996). Benchmarking the generalization capabilities of a compiling genetic programming system using sparse data sets. In Koza, J. R., Goldberg, D. E., Fogel, D. B., and Riolo, R. L., editors, *Genetic Programming 1996: Proceedings of the First Annual Conference*, pages 72–80, Stanford University, CA, USA. MIT Press.

Freeman, J. J. (1998). A linear representation for GP using context free grammars. In Koza, J. R., Banzhaf, W., Chellapilla, K., Deb, K., Dorigo, M., Fogel, D. B., Garzon, M. H., Goldberg, D. E., Iba, H., and Riolo, R., editors, *Genetic Programming 1998: Proceedings of the Third Annual Conference*, pages 72–77, University of Wisconsin, Madison, Wisconsin, USA. Morgan Kaufmann.

Friedberg, R. (1958). A learning machine: Part 1. *IBM J. Research and Development*, Vol. 2:1:2–13.

Friedberg, R., Dunham, B., and North, J. (1959). A learning machine: Part 2. *IBM J. Research and Development*, pages 282–287.

GE. (2003). grammatical-evolution.org. http://www.grammatical-evolution.org.

Geyer-Schulz, A. (1995). *Fuzzy Rule-Based Expert Systems and Genetic Machine Learning*, volume 3 of *Studies in Fuzziness*. Physica-Verlag, Heidelberg, Germany.

Geyer-Schulz, A. (1997). The next 700 programming languages for genetic programming. In Koza, J. R., Deb, K., Dorigo, M., Fogel, D. B., Garzon, M., Iba, H., and Riolo, R. L., editors, *Genetic Programming 1997: Proceedings of the Second Annual Conference*, pages 128–136, Stanford University, CA, USA. Morgan Kaufmann.

Goldberg, D. (1987). Nonstationary function optimisation with dominance and diploidy. In *Second International Conference on Genetic Algorithms*.

Goldberg, D. (1989). *Genetic Algorithms in Search, Optimization and Machine Learning*. Addison Wesley.

Goldberg, D. (2002). *The Design of Innovation: Lessons from and for Competent Genetic Algorithms*. Genetic Algorithms and Evolutionary Computation. Kluwer Academic Publishers.

Goldberg, D., Deb, K., and Korb, B. (1991a). Don't worry, be messy. In Belew, R. and Booker, L., editors, *Proceedings of the Fourth International Conference on Genetic Algorithms*, pages 24–30. Morgan Kaufmann.

Goldberg, D., Deb, K., and Korb, B. (1991b). Don't worry, be messy. In Belew, R. and Booker, L., editors, *Proceedings of the Fourth International Conference on Genetic Algorithms*, pages 24–30. Morgan Kaufmann.

Goldberg, D., Korb, B., and Deb, K. (1989). Messy genetic algorithms: motivation, analysis, and first results. *Complex Systems*, 3:493–530.

Gruau, F. (1994). *Neural Network Synthesis using Cellular Encoding and the Genetic Algorithm.* PhD thesis, Laboratoire de l'Informatique du Parallilisme, Ecole Normale Supirieure de Lyon, France.

Harik, G. (1999). Linkage learning via probabilistic modeling in the ecga. Technical Report IlliGAL Report No. 99010, University of Illinois at Urbana-Champaign.

Harik, G. and Goldberg, D. (1997). Learning linkage. In Belew, R. and Vose, M. D., editors, *Foundations of Genetic Algorithms 4*, pages 247–262. Morgan Kaufmann.

Haynes, T. (1996). Duplication of coding segments in genetic programming. In *Proceedings of the Thirteenth National Conference on Artificial Intelligence*, pages 344–349, Portland, OR.

Holland, J. H. (1975). *Adaptation in Natural and Artificial Systems.* University of Michigan Press.

Hollstein, R. (1971). *Artificial genetic adaptation in computer control systems.* PhD thesis, University of Michigan.

Horner, H. (1996). A C++ class library for genetic programming: The vienna university of economics genetic programming kernel. Vienna University of Economics.

Huynen, M. (1995). Exploring phenotype space through neutral evolution. Technical Report 95-10-100, Santa Fe Institute.

Huynen, M., Stadler, P., and Fontana, W. (1996). Smoothness within ruggedness: the role of neutrality in apdaptation. *Proc. Natl. Acad. Sci. (USA)*, 93:397–401.

Iba, H. and Nikolaev, N. (2000). Genetic programming polynomial models of financial data series. In *Proc. of CEC 2000*, pages 1459–1466. IEEE Press.

IlliGAL (2003). IlliGAL website. http://www-illigal.ge.uiuc.edu/.

Jacob, F. and Monod, J. (1961). Genetic regulatory mechanisms in the synthesis of proteins. *Journal of Molecular Biology*, 3:318–356.

Kargupta, H. (1997). Relation learning in gene expression: Introns, variable length representation, and all that. Position paper at the Workshop on Exploring Non-coding Segments and Genetics-based Encodings at ICGA-97.

Kargupta, H. (1998). Revisiting the gemga: Scalable evolutionary optimization through linkage learning. In *Proc. of IEEE International Conference on Evolutionary Computation*, pages 603–608. IEEE Press.

Kargupta, H., Deb, K., and Goldberg, D. (1992). Ordering genetic algorithms and deceptions. In et al, E., editor, *Parallel Problem Solving from Nature - PPSN II*, pages 47–56.

Kargupta, H. and Sarkar, K. (1999). Function induction, gene expression, and evolutionary representation construction. In Banzhaf, W., Daida, J., Eiben, A. E., Garzon, M. H., Honavar, V., Jakiela, M., and Smith, R. E., editors, *Proceedings of the Genetic and Evolutionary Computation Conference*, volume 1, pages 313–320, Orlando, Florida, USA. Morgan Kaufmann.

Keijzer, M. (2002). *Scientific Discovery using Genetic Programming.* PhD thesis, Technical University of Denmark.

Keijzer, M., Babovic, V., Ryan, C., O'Neill, M., and Cattolico, M. (2001a). Adaptive logic programming. In *Proceedings of the Genetic and Evolutionary Computation Conference - GECCO 2001*, pages 42–49. Morgan Kaufmann.

Keijzer, M., Ryan, C., O'Neill, M., Cattolico, M., and Babovic, V. (2001b). Ripple crossover in genetic programming. In *Proceedings of EuroGP 2001.*

Keith, M. J. and Martin, M. C. (1994). Genetic programming in C++: Implementation issues. In Kinnear, Jr., K. E., editor, *Advances in Genetic Programming*, chapter 13, pages 285–310. MIT Press.

Keller, R. E. and Banzhaf, W. (1996). Genetic programming using genotype-phenotype mapping from linear genomes into linear phenotypes. In Koza, J. R., Goldberg, D. E., Fogel, D. B., and Riolo, R. L., editors, *Genetic Programming 1996: Proceedings of the First Annual Conference*, pages 116–122, Stanford University, CA, USA. MIT Press.

Keller, R. E. and Banzhaf, W. (1999). The evolution of genetic code in genetic programming. In Banzhaf, W., Daida, J., Eiben, A. E., Garzon, M. H., Honavar, V., Jakiela, M., and Smith, R. E., editors, *Proceedings of the Genetic and Evolutionary Computation Conference*, volume 2, pages 1077–1082, Orlando, Florida, USA. Morgan Kaufmann.

Keller, R. E. and Banzhaf, W. (2001). Evolution of genetic code on a hard problem. In Spector, L., Goodman, E. D., Wu, A., Langdon, W. B., Voigt, H.-M., Gen, M., Sen, S., Dorigo, M., Pezeshk, S., Garzon, M. H., and Burke, E., editors, *Proceedings of the Genetic and Evolutionary Computation Conference (GECCO-2001)*, pages 50–56, San Francisco, California, USA. Morgan Kaufmann.

Kennedy, P. J. (1998). *Simulation of the Evolution of Single Celled Organisms with Genome, Metabolism and Time-Varying Phenotype*. PhD thesis, University of Technology, Sydney.

Kimura, M. (1983). *The Neutral Theory of Molecular Evolution*. Cambridge University Press.

Kinnear, Jr., K. E., editor (1994). *Advances in Genetic Programming*. MIT Press, Cambridge, MA.

Knjazew, D. and Goldberg, D. (2000). Omega - ordering messy ga : Solving problems with the fast messy genetic algorithm and random keys. In et al, W., editor, *GECCO-2000: Proceedings of the Genetic and Evolutionary Computation Conference*, pages 181–199.

Knuth, D. E. (1964). Backus normal form vs. backus naur form. *Communications of the ACM*, 7(12):735–736.

Koza, J. R. (1989). Hierarchical genetic algorithms operating on populations of computer programs. In Sridharan, N., editor, *Proceedings of the 11th International Conference on Artificial Intelligence*, pages 768–774. Morgan Kaufmann.

Koza, J. R. (1992). *Genetic Programming: On the Programming of Computers by Means of Natural Selection*. MIT Press, Cambridge, MA, USA.

Koza, J. R. (1994). *Genetic Programming II: Automatic Discovery of Reusable Programs*. MIT Press, Cambridge Massachusetts.

Koza, J. R. (2000). www.genetic-programming.org: A source of information about the field of genetic programming. http://www.genetic-programming.org.

Koza, J. R., David Andre, Bennett III, F. H., and Keane, M. (1999). *Genetic Programming 3: Darwinian Invention and Problem Solving*. Morgan Kaufman.

Langdon, W. B. (1998). *Data Structures and Genetic Programming: Genetic Programming + Data Structures = Automatic Programming!*, volume 1 of *Genetic Programming*. Kluwer, Boston.

Langdon, W. B. (1999). Size fair and homologous tree genetic programming crossovers. In Banzhaf, W., Daida, J., Eiben, A. E., Garzon, M. H., Honavar, V., Jakiela, M., and Smith, R. E., editors, *Proceedings of the Genetic and Evolutionary Computation Conference*, volume 2, pages 1092–1097, Orlando, Florida, USA. Morgan Kaufmann.

Langdon, W. B. (2000). Size fair and homologous tree genetic programming crossovers. *Genetic Programming And Evolvable Machines*, 1(1/2):95–119.

Langdon, W. B. and Koza, J. R. (2003). GP Bibliography. http://www.cs.bham.ac.uk/ wbl/biblio/gp-bib-info.html.

Langdon, W. B. and Poli, R. (1998). Why ants are hard. In Koza, J. R., Banzhaf, W., Chellapilla, K., Deb, K., Dorigo, M., Fogel, D. B., Garzon, M. H., Goldberg, D. E., Iba, H., and Riolo, R., editors, *Genetic Programming 1998: Proceedings of the Third Annual Conference*, pages 193–201, University of Wisconsin, Madison, Wisconsin, USA. Morgan Kaufmann.

Levenick, J. R. (1991). Inserting introns improves genetic algorithm success rate: Taking a cue from biology. In Belew, R. and Booker, L., editors, *Proceedings of the 4th International Conference on Genetic Algorithms*, pages 123–127, San Diego, CA.

Levenick, J. R. (1999). Swappers: Introns promote flexibility, diversity and invention. In Banzhaf, W., Daida, J., Eiben, A. E., Garzon, M. H., Honavar, V., Jakiela, M., and Smith, R. E., editors,

Proceedings of the Genetic and Evolutionary Computation Conference, volume 1, pages 361–368, Orlando, Florida, USA. Morgan Kaufmann.

Lewin, B. (1999). *Genes VII*. Oxford University Press.

Lobo, F. G., Deb, K., Goldberg, D. E., Harik, G. R., and Wang, L. (1998). Compressed introns in a linkage learning genetic algorithm. In Koza, J. R., Banzhaf, W., Chellapilla, K., Deb, K., Dorigo, M., Fogel, D. B., Garzon, M. H., Goldberg, D. E., Iba, H., and Riolo, R., editors, *Genetic Programming 1998: Proceedings of the Third Annual Conference*, pages 551–558, University of Wisconsin, Madison, Wisconsin, USA. Morgan Kaufmann.

Lovely, R. (1992). Loft: A tool for automatic parallelisation of Fortran programs. In Valero, M., Onate, E., Jane, M., Larriba, J. L., and Suarez, B., editors, *Parallel Computing and Transputer Applications*, pages 277–286, Amsterdam, The Netherlands. IOS Press.

Miller, J. F. and Thomson, P. (2000). Cartesian genetic programming. In Poli, R., Banzhaf, W., Langdon, W. B., Miller, J. F., Nordin, P., and Fogarty, T. C., editors, *Genetic Programming, Proceedings of EuroGP'2000*, volume 1802 of *LNCS*, pages 121–132, Edinburgh. Springer-Verlag.

Montana, D. J. (1995). Strongly typed genetic programming. *Evolutionary Computation*, 3(2):199–230.

Muggleton, S., editor (1992). *Inductive logic programming*. London : Academic.

Murphy, J. J. (1999). *Technical Analysis of the Financial Markets*. New York Institute of Finance, New York.

Naur, P. (1963). Revised report on the algorithmic language algol 60. *Communications of the ACM*, 6(1):1–17.

Nelson, T. (1999). Investigations into the master mind board game. http://www.tnelson.demon.co.uk/mastermind/index.html.

Newman, M. and Engelhardt, R. (1998). Effects of neutral selection on the evolution of molecular species. *Proc. R. Soc. London B*.

Ng, K. and Wong, K. (1995). A new diploid scheme and dominance change mechanism for non-stationary function optimisation. In *Fifth International Conference on Genetic Algorithms*.

Nordin, P. (1994). A compiling genetic programming system that directly manipulates the machine code. In Kinnear, Jr., K. E., editor, *Advances in Genetic Programming*, chapter 14, pages 311–331. MIT Press.

Nordin, P. (1997). *Evolutionary Program Induction of Binary Machine Code and its Applications*. PhD thesis, der Universitat Dortmund am Fachereich Informatik.

Nordin, P. (1998). AIMGP: A formal description. In Koza, J. R., editor, *Late Breaking Papers at the Genetic Programming 1998 Conference*, University of Wisconsin, Madison, Wisconsin, USA. Stanford University Bookstore.

Nordin, P. and Banzhaf, W. (1995a). Complexity compression and evolution. In Eshelman, L., editor, *Genetic Algorithms: Proceedings of the Sixth International Conference (ICGA95)*, pages 310–317, Pittsburgh, PA, USA. Morgan Kaufmann.

Nordin, P. and Banzhaf, W. (1995b). Evolving turing-complete programs for a register machine with self-modifying code. In Eshelman, L., editor, *Genetic Algorithms: Proceedings of the Sixth International Conference (ICGA95)*, pages 318–325, Pittsburgh, PA, USA. Morgan Kaufmann.

Nordin, P., Banzhaf, W., and Francone, F. D. (1999). Efficient evolution of machine code for CISC architectures using instruction blocks and homologous crossover. In Spector, L., Langdon, W. B., O'Reilly, U.-M., and Angeline, P. J., editors, *Advances in Genetic Programming 3*, chapter 12, pages 275–299. MIT Press, Cambridge, MA, USA.

Nordin, P., Francone, F., and Banzhaf, W. (1996). Explicitly defined introns and destructive crossover in genetic programming. In Angeline, P. J. and Kinnear, Jr., K. E., editors, *Advances in Genetic Programming 2*, chapter 6, pages 111–134. MIT Press, Cambridge, MA, USA.

Olsson, J. R. (1994). *Inductive functional programming using incremental program transformation and Execution of logic programs by iterative-deepening A* SLD-tree search.* PhD thesis, University of Oslo.

Olsson, J. R. (1995). Inductive functional programming using incremental program transformation. *Artificial Intelligence*, 74(1):55–83.

Olsson, J. R. (1999). How to invent functions. In Poli, R., Nordin, P., Langdon, W. B., and Fogarty, T. C., editors, *Genetic Programming, Proceedings of EuroGP'99*, volume 1598 of *LNCS*, pages 232–243, Goteborg, Sweden. Springer-Verlag.

O'Neill, M. (2001). *Evolutionary Automatic Programming in an Arbitrary Language: Evolving Programs with Grammatical Evolution.* PhD thesis, University Of Limerick.

O'Neill, M., Brabazon, A., and Ryan, C. (2002). Forecasting market indices using evolutionary automatic programming: A case study. In Chen, S.-H., editor, *Genetic Algorithms and Genetic Programming in Economics and Finance.* Kluwer Academic Publishers.

O'Neill, M., Brabazon, A., Ryan, C., and Collins, J. (2001a). Developing a market timing system using grammatical evolution. In Spector, L., Goodman, E. D., Wu, A., Langdon, W. B., Voigt, H.-M., Gen, M., Sen, S., Dorigo, M., Pezeshk, S., Garzon, M. H., and Burke, E., editors, *Proceedings of the Genetic and Evolutionary Computation Conference (GECCO-2001)*, pages 1375–1381, San Francisco, California, USA. Morgan Kaufmann.

O'Neill, M., Brabazon, A., Ryan, C., and Collins, J. J. (2001b). Evolving market index trading rules using grammatical evolution. In Boers, E. J. W., Cagnoni, S., Gottlieb, J., Hart, E., Lanzi, P. L., Raidl, G. R., Smith, R. E., and Tijink, H., editors, *Applications of Evolutionary Computing*, volume 2037 of *LNCS*, pages 343–352, Lake Como, Italy. Springer-Verlag.

O'Neill, M. and Ryan, C. (1999a). Automatic generation of caching algorithms. In Miettinen, K., Mäkelä, M. M., Neittaanmäki, P., and Periaux, J., editors, *Evolutionary Algorithms in Engineering and Computer Science*, pages 127–134, Jyväskylä, Finland. John Wiley & Sons.

O'Neill, M. and Ryan, C. (1999b). Genetic code degeneracy: Implications for grammatical evolution and beyond. In *ECAL'99: Proc. of the Fifth European Conference on Artificial Life*, Lausanne, Switzerland.

O'Neill, M. and Ryan, C. (2000). Grammar based function definition in grammatical evolution. In Whitley, D., Goldberg, D., Cantú-Paz, E., Spector, L., Parmee, I., and Beyer., H.-G., editors, *GECCO 2000: Proc. of the Genetic & Evolutionary Computation Conference*, pages 485–490, Las Vegas, Nevada. Morgan Kaufmann.

O'Neill, M. and Ryan, C. (2001). Grammatical Evolution. *IEEE Transactions on Evolutionary Computation*, 5(4).

O'Neill, M., Ryan, C., Keijzer, M., and Cattolico, M. (2003). Crossover in grammatical evolution. *Genetic Programming and Evolvable Machines*, 4(1).

O'Neill, M., Ryan, C., and Nicolau, M. (2001c). Grammar defined introns: An investigation into grammars, introns, and bias in grammatical evolution. In Spector, L., Goodman, E. D., Wu, A., Langdon, W. B., Voigt, H.-M., Gen, M., Sen, S., Dorigo, M., Pezeshk, S., Garzon, M. H., and Burke, E., editors, *Proceedings of the Genetic and Evolutionary Computation Conference (GECCO-2001)*, pages 97–103, San Francisco, California, USA. Morgan Kaufmann.

O'Sullivan, J. (2003). An investigation into the use of different search strategies with grammatical evolution. Master's thesis, University of Limerick, Ireland.

O'Sullivan, J. and Ryan, C. (2002). An investigation into ge search strategies. In *Proceedings of EuroGP 2002.*

Ošmera, P., Kvasnička, V., and Pospíchal, J. (1997). Genetic algorithms with diploid chromosomes. In *Proceedings of Mendel '97, 3rd International Mendel Conference on Genetic Algorithms, Fuzzy Logic, Neural Networks, and Rough Sets*, pages 111–116, Brno, Czech Republic.

Paterson, N. and Livesey, M. (1997). Evolving caching algorithms in C by genetic programming. In Koza, J. R., Deb, K., Dorigo, M., Fogel, D. B., Garzon, M., Iba, H., and Riolo, R. L., editors, *Genetic Programming 1997: Proceedings of the Second Annual Conference*, pages 262–267, Stanford University, CA, USA. Morgan Kaufmann.

Paterson, N. R. and Livesey, M. (1996). Distinguishing genotype and phenotype in genetic programming. In Koza, J. R., editor, *Late Breaking Papers at the Genetic Programming 1996 Conference Stanford University July 28-31, 1996*, pages 141–150, Stanford University, CA, USA. Stanford Bookstore.

Paton, R. (1994). Enhancing evolutionary computation using analogues of biological mechanisms. In Fogarty, T., editor, *Lecture Notes in Computer Science 865, Evolutionary Computing*, pages 51–64. Springer.

Paton, R. (1997). Principles of genetics. In *Handbook of Evolutionary Computation*. IOP Publishing Ltd., and Oxford University Press.

Pelikan, M., Goldberg, D., and Cantú-Paz, E. (2000). Linkage problem, distribution estimation, and bayesian networks. *Evolutionary Computation*, 8(3):311–340.

Poli, R. and Langdon, W. B. (1998). On the search properties of different crossover operators in genetic programming. In Koza, J. R., Banzhaf, W., Chellapilla, K., Deb, K., Dorigo, M., Fogel, D. B., Garzon, M. H., Goldberg, D. E., Iba, H., and Riolo, R., editors, *Genetic Programming 1998: Proceedings of the Third Annual Conference*, pages 293–301, University of Wisconsin, Madison, Wisconsin, USA. Morgan Kaufmann.

Pring, M. (1991). *Technical analysis explained: the successful investor's guide to spotting investment trends and turning points*. Mc Graw-Hill.

Quinlan, J. (1990). Learning logical definitions from relations. *Machine Learning*, 5:239–266.

Reidys, C. (1995). *Neutral Networks of RNA Secondary-strcutures*. PhD thesis, Friedrich Schiller Universität Jena.

Reidys, C., Forst, C., and Schuster, P. (1998). Replication and mutation on neutral networks of rna secondary structures. *Bull. Math. Biol.* In Press, Santa Fe Institute Preprint 98-04-036.

Reidys, C., Stadler, P., and Schuster, P. (1997). Generic properties of combinatory maps - neutral networks of rna secondary structures. *Bull. Math. Biol.*, 59:339–337.

Rich, C. and Waters, R. (1988). Automatic programming: Myths and prospects. *IEEE Computer*, pages 40–51.

RML Technologies (1998). Discipulus. http://www.aimlearning.com.

Ryan, C. (1996). *Reducing Premature Convergence in Evolutionary Algorithms*. PhD thesis, University College, Cork, Ireland.

Ryan, C. (1999). *Automatic Re-engineering of Software Using Genetic Programming*, volume 2 of *Genetic Programming*. Kluwer Academic Publishers.

Ryan, C., Azad, A., Sheahan, A., and O'Neill, M. (2002a). No coercion and no prohibition, A position independent encoding scheme for evolutionary algorithms—the Chorus system. In Foster, J. A., Lutton, E., Miller, J., Ryan, C., and Tettamanzi, A. G. B., editors, *Genetic Programming, Proceedings of the 5th European Conference, EuroGP 2002*, volume 2278 of *LNCS*, pages 131–141, Kinsale, Ireland. Springer-Verlag.

Ryan, C. and Collins, J. (1998). Polygenic inheritance - a haploid scheme that can outperform diploidy. In *Fifth Int. Conf. on Parallel Problem Solving from Nature*, LNCS 1498, pages 178–187, Amsterdam. Springer.

Ryan, C., Collins, J., and O'Neill, M. (1998). Grammatical evolution: Evolving programs for an arbitrary language. In Banzhaf, W., Poli, R., Schoenauer, M., and Fogarty, T. C., editors, *Proceedings of the First European Workshop on Genetic Programming*, volume 1391 of *LNCS*, pages 83–95, Paris. Springer-Verlag.

Ryan, C. and Ivan, L. (1999). An automatice software re-engineering tool based on genetic programming. In Spector, L., Langdon, W. B., O'Reilly, U.-M., and Angeline, P. J., editors,

Advances in Genetic Programming 3, chapter 2, pages 15–39. MIT Press, Cambridge, MA, USA.

Ryan, C., Nicolau, M., and O'Neill, M. (2002b). Genetic algorithms using grammatical evolution. In Foster, J. A., Lutton, E., Miller, J., Ryan, C., and Tettamanzi, A. G. B., editors, *Genetic Programming, Proceedings of the 5th European Conference, EuroGP 2002*, volume 2278 of *LNCS*, pages 278–287, Kinsale, Ireland. Springer-Verlag.

Ryan, C. and Walsh, P. (1997). The evolution of provable parallel programs. In Koza, J. R., Deb, K., Dorigo, M., Fogel, D. B., Garzon, M., Iba, H., and Riolo, R. L., editors, *Genetic Programming 1997: Proceedings of the Second Annual Conference*, pages 295–302, Stanford University, CA, USA. Morgan Kaufmann.

Salustowicz, R. P. and Schmidhuber, J. (1997). Probabilistic incremental program evolution. *Evolutionary Computation*, 5(2):123–141.

Samuel, A. L. (1959). Some studies in machine learning using the game of checkers. *IBM Journal of Research and Development*, 3(3):210–229.

Sheehan, L. (2000). Ecoga : a novel self-adapting ecologically inspired genetic algorithm. Master's thesis, University of Limerick.

Smith, P. W. H. and Harries, K. (1998). Code growth, explicitly defined introns, and alternative selection schemes. *Evolutionary Computation*, 6(4):339–360.

Spector, L., Langdon, W. B., O'Reilly, U.-M., and Angeline, P. J., editors (1999). *Advances in Genetic Programming 3*. MIT Press, Cambridge, MA, USA.

Spencer, H. (1864). *The Principles of Biology*, volume 1. Williams and Norgate, London and Edinburgh.

Sterling, L. and Shapiro, E. (1994). *The Art of Prolog*. MIT press.

Teller, A. (1994). The evolution of mental models. In Kinnear, Jr., K. E., editor, *Advances in Genetic Programming*, chapter 9, pages 199–219. MIT Press.

Thierens, D. (1999). Scalability problems of simple genetic algorithms. *Evolutionary Computation*, 7(4):331–352.

van Nimwegen, E. and Crutchfield, J. P. (1999). Neutral evolution of mutational robustness. Technical Report 99-03-021, Santa Fe Institute.

Vassilev, V. and Miller, J. (2000). The advantages of landscape neutrality in digital circuit evolution. In *ICES 2000. Evolvable Systems: From Biology to Hardware*, pages 252–263, Edinburgh, Scotland.

Whigham, P. A. (1995a). Grammatically-based genetic programming. In Rosca, J. P., editor, *Proceedings of the Workshop on Genetic Programming: From Theory to Real-World Applications*, pages 33–41, Tahoe City, California, USA.

Whigham, P. A. (1995b). Inductive bias and genetic programming. In Zalzala, A. M. S., editor, *First International Conference on Genetic Algorithms in Engineering Systems: Innovations and Applications, GALESIA*, volume 414, pages 461–466, Sheffield, UK. IEE.

Whigham, P. A. (1996a). *Grammatical Bias for Evolutionary Learning*. PhD thesis, School of Computer Science, University College, University of New South Wales, Australian Defence Force Academy.

Whigham, P. A. (1996b). Search bias, language bias, and genetic programming. In Koza, J. R., Goldberg, D. E., Fogel, D. B., and Riolo, R. L., editors, *Genetic Programming 1996: Proceedings of the First Annual Conference*, pages 230–237, Stanford University, CA, USA. MIT Press.

Wineberg, M. and Oppacher, F. (1996). The benefits of computing with introns. In Koza, J. R., Goldberg, D. E., Fogel, D. B., and Riolo, R. L., editors, *Genetic Programming 1996: Proceedings of the First Annual Conference*, pages 410–415, Stanford University, CA, USA. MIT Press.

Wong, M. L. (1995). *Evolutionary Program Induction Directed by Logic Grammars*. PhD thesis, Department of Computer Science and Engineering. The Chinese University of Hong Kong.

Wong, M. L. and Leung, K. S. (1994). Inductive logic programming using genetic algorithms. In Brahan, J. W. and Lasker, G. E., editors, *Advances in Artificial Intelligence - Theory and Application II*, pages 119–124. I.I.A.S., Ontario, Canada.

Wong, M. L. and Leung, K. S. (1995). Applying logic grammars to induce sub-functions in genetic programming. In *1995 IEEE Conference on Evolutionary Computation*, volume 2, pages 737–740, Perth, Australia. IEEE Press.

Wong, M. L. and Leung, K. S. (1997). Evolutionary program induction directed by logic grammars. *Evolutionary Computation*, 5(2):143–180.

Wong, M. L. and Leung, K. S. (2000). *Data Mining Using Grammar Based Genetic Programming and Applications*, volume 3 of *Genetic Programming*. Kluwer Academic Publishers.

Wu, A. S. and Lindsay, R. K. (1995). Empirical studies of the genetic algorithm with noncoding segments. *Evolutionary Computation*, 3:121–148.

Wu, A. S. and Lindsay, R. K. (1996). A survey of intron research in genetics. In Voigt, H.-M., Ebeling, W., Rechenberg, I., and Schwefel, H.-P., editors, *Parallel Problem Solving From Nature IV. Proceedings of the International Conference on Evolutionary Computation*, volume 1141 of *LNCS*, pages 101–110, Berlin, Germany. Springer-Verlag.

Yu, T. and Bentley, P. (1998). Methods to evolve legal phenotypes. In Eiben, A. E., Back, T., Schoenauer, M., and Schwefel, H.-P., editors, *Fifth International Conference on Parallel Problem Solving from Nature*, volume 1498 of *LNCS*, pages 280–291, Amsterdam. Springer.

Index